I0416228

Revolutionary Retailing

The Complete "Wise Guys" Guide to Small Business Management and Marketing

by

Robert Kramer
The Revolutionary Retailer ™

authorHOUSE

1663 LIBERTY DRIVE, SUITE 200
BLOOMINGTON, INDIANA 47403
(800) 839-8640
www.authorhouse.com

© 2004 Robert Kramer, The Revolutionary Retailer ™.
All Rights Reserved.

No part of this book may be reproduced, stored in a retrieval system, or transmitted by any means without the written permission of the author.

First published by AuthorHouse 06/11/04

ISBN: 1-4184-1658-4 (e)
ISBN: 1-4184-1657-6 (sc)

This book is printed on acid-free paper.

ACKNOWLEDGEMENTS

I want to thank the people who enabled me to get this book completed in less than thirty years!

The National Speakers Association, especially my fifty closest author/speaker/friends, I thank you, individually, for your encouragement in telling me to "put it in a book."

Fellow business consultants and business owners too numerous to mention, I thank you for your feedback and suggestions during the construction of this manuscript.

Matt Stadelman and **Becky Gillespie**, honor students in the Miami University School of Business, I envy your future employer! Thank you both for your assistance, suggestions and motivational tickles in pushing Revolutionary Retailing to a roaring conclusion in the final six months.

Gerdean Bowen, my wonderful editor, I thank you for working with me to make the manuscript as reader-friendly as possible. Check her out: www.ZooidMission.com.

Mr. Dave Goodman, my business partner of 25-years plus, referred to frequently (and rightfully) in this text as an integral part of my business success, I sincerely thank you.

Lois, my wife of 28 years, daughter **Mindee**, and son **Todd**, I thank you, for making me proud. And **Muffin**, **Muggsy**, and **Hershey**, for the indulgences.

Dedicated to
Fond Memories of

DAD & MOM KRAMER

TABLE OF CONTENTS

FOREWORD

REVOLUTIONARY RETAILING

How can the small independent retailer win the retail war against the giant national discount chains and mass merchants? According to Bob Kramer, one need only think back to how the Revolutionary War was won, then emulate the spirit and tactics of the colonial soldiers.

The British army, like big business, naturally had much superior training and resources. The patriot soldiers could have allowed themselves to be discouraged because of the apparently overwhelming odds against them, just as many small retailers have been intimidated right out of business by the retail giants. But they didn't admit defeat. Rather than wasting all their energy "whining" about the advantages the British had, with their big guns and naval cannon power, the patriots focused on "winning." They identified the weaknesses of their adversary.

The British were predictable in every move they made. Their distance from the home base made it difficult for them to keep their troops supplied. Their command structure could not react quickly enough to the rapidly changing battle situation in each local area. In short, all the financial resources of the British Empire were no match for the clever strategies of the rebels. Superior firepower meant little when the British stood out in the open, exposed, while the patriots took calculated aim from behind the trees.

To win the retail war, the independent operator has to be smart, quick tough, aggressive, innovative and shrewd. The small retailer must learn to out-think, rather than out-spend the competition. Winning the battle is a matter of brains over bucks.

In the past, when a major competitor of mine advertised vacuum cleaners below his cost and mine I would get discouraged. It seemed unfair because I suspected the manufacturer was underwriting the ad to such an extent that my competitor was making a profit *on the ad.* I lamented that he most likely got the supplier to pay for 75% of his in-house ad agency preparation charges, highly inflated, and added that to the ad co-op, letting him be "paid" over 100% of the ad cost. Money for nothing!

When I decided to put some action into my reaction; it gave me satisfaction! I felt much better and had more fun. Now, I am there when that store opens and I buy the entire inventory. I present my resale certificate to avoid paying tax. Guessing the store must enjoy selling goods below cost, I used my American Express card to make them and me a few percentage points happier.

What did I accomplish by this? Lots:
1)   I am no longer intimidated by my competition because I have discovered my competition's incompetence! In this case, he referred me to a salesman who was in charge of the vac department, but the only way he could identify the advertised model was by matching the model number in the ad with the hang tags on the vacs. He made no attempt to show any other models.
2)   I removed his entire inventory so he would have very unhappy customers the rest of the day. Shoppers would leave his store mad, and in a hurry! Since the advertised model was unavailable, they were convinced it was all just a come-on.
3)   I got some low end merchandise below my wholesale cost, paid no freight, and didn't have to buy eighteen to get the free key chain being offered that month.
4)   It was cheaper for us to buy them retail, which my sales rep learned when he found out we didn't need any vacs from him

anymore.

5)   I almost forgot to mention that I got a bonus of 18 packs of bags free.

6)   And, I had fun.

Here's another example: A large retailer spends over $7,000.00 to advertise a single model of a vac that was going to earn him about $12 per unit gross profit. It was advertised to be on sale for 3 days only for $188.00. An ad like that used to get to me because I didn't have $7,000.00 to spend, nor did I have the clout to kick in towards it. But I could think! It was such a nice ad, I decided to use it in my store. It worked for my competitor for 3 days; I used it effectively for over 6 months.

I mounted the ad on poster board and hung it on a display of the advertised model right at my cash register. I used a big bright orange burst overlay to state that our everyday low price is only $178.00, or $10.00 less than the super discount center's three-day sale price. Everyone who stopped in for bags or belts left our store "knowing" that we charge less than the major discount store in the market. Guess where they will they buy their next vac? Yes, we are cheaper … on that model. We didn't sell very many, but we were willing. For each one that sold, 50 other customers selected an alternate brand at the same price with better features — better features on the vacuum for the customer and the feature of better profitability for me.

Yes, it is your choice. You can use your energy to worry about the competition or you can decide to use your energy to BE the competition. Whenever your big gun competitor does something to discourage you, just remember the formula

$$A + B = C$$

The Consequences equal the Adversity plus your Beliefs about it. Your beliefs will determine 90% of the outcome.

Negative thinking creates an "enter manure" where you lack social fragrance and your business rolls downhill. But positive thinking, and reacting with positive action, creates an "entrepreneur" where you are advancing, ascending and winning – the Revolutionary Retailing way!

INTRODUCTION

Before my fingers hit the keyboard to type the first word of this book, my editor wanted to know where it would take you, the reader. Tongue in cheek, I quipped, "This book is going to take the reader every step of the way through the maze of commerce to become a successful small business."

Perhaps I was lucky to find an editor with such an off-the-wall perspective, because she came back with, "Can you explain to us how we can hold onto our assets when, in our fur coat and jewels, we drive our limousine down to the courthouse to file bankruptcy?"

The sad truth, according to U.S. Government data, is that most start-up businesses *do* end with bankruptcy as their final chapter, and it is not at all glamorous. Fewer in number, but equally sad, are the many, many existing businesses and businesses transferred to new owners, which ultimately fail.

On June 8, 1972, I purchased from my father the retail store he had founded in 1947. Subsequently, I built that enterprise into a small chain of stores, some successful, some not. I won't lie to you: you will learn from my triumphs as well as my tragedies! Even though I sold my last location on September 7, 1999, all the stores are still prospering and still growing sales … fifty-seven years after the door of the first store swung open for the first customer.

In the twenty-six years that I owned and operated Kramer's Sew and Vac stores, the one thing I have learned over and over is that you get smart by doing dumb things. I hope that by sharing with you some of the mistakes I have made and observed, you might possibly be able to skip some of the common pitfalls. You see, to be successful in business requires that you exercise good judgment in all of your decisions. Unfortunately, the way you develop good judgment is with experience, which is what you get when you have used bad judgment.

I started with a single store when I was twenty-two years old and had three more by the time I was twenty-nine, and was convinced I had a good shot at being general manager of the universe by the time I was forty. I recently sold my last two stores and today, at fifty-four, I am much smarter than I was thirty-two years ago. Kramer's Sew & Vac Centers have provided me with a very comfortable livelihood and lifestyle, allowing me to retire at age fifty.

I hope you are asking yourself, *"What did Bob do?"* My singular purpose in writing this book is to answer that question in the simplest terms possible. Briefly, I did it by hiring some top talent early on. I treated my employees fairly, with respect and appreciation, so that some key people stayed with me for over 25 years and are still active in the business! I let my associates carry me through some tough times when I felt frustrated and burned out. I promoted our business aggressively but always within a budget that made sense, related to our current sales and our future sales goals. I used mind power rather than money power to compete with the giants. And I did it in 47 other ways!

Fair warning to the established business owners who have read this far: You are headed straight for "Chapter 13" if you skimmed the chapter headings and dismissed chapters one through four. If you thought, "I can skip part one of this book because I have already made those decisions," please think again. Did you *decide* where to locate your business last year? If you answered "No" then "Bzzzzt!" is my response. You decide each and every year by default. If you did not consider changing your organizational structure, the store location, and store manager last year you still *made a choice.*

These non-choice choices often turn out to be the most nefarious kind because they are silent killers that strike while we are asleep at the helm. Please read Part I. The worst result is that your active or non-decisions can be affirmed. The best result is that these non-decisions can be reviewed to keep your business on course to enjoy the fifty-seven years of success that the Kramer family has enjoyed and continues to enjoy. Stay alert; be on guard for creeping paralysis. I have seen it cripple many a business.

You will learn the 47 other ways to make your small business succeed if you read all the way from Chapter 1 to the final Chapter, where I conclude by sharing how I successfully sold my thriving store locations to provide a healthy income stream for up to ten years after my retirement from retail. I hope that you can do the same, when you so choose. "Bank depositing" is more fun than bankrupting.

— Bob Kramer, The Revolutionary Retailer

PART I –

GETTING STARTED

Chapter 1
BUSINESS STRUCTURE

One of the first determinations you make in starting a business is how to legally structure your operation. Will you operate as a proprietorship, a corporation, a partnership, or a limited liability company?

Making this decision can be confusing. (If you are confused, you should talk to your attorney. If you are *not* confused, it is because you haven't talked to your attorney yet! Ha!) I would suggest that you operate as a proprietorship until such time as you have a valid reason to choose a different structure. Several possible reasons are discussed below.

When I took over my father's business, I continued to run it as a proprietorship for the first year. I probably would have operated a simple proprietorship for much longer if it were not for specific legal complications that arose from operating in a dual mode as both a wholesale distributor and as a retail dealer for Viking sewing machines. When I separated my wholesale and retail businesses, I went with the traditional C type corporation, the type used by the giant corporations of America. I needed to accumulate working capital for this brand new entity and it was much easier to do this at the C corporate tax rate of 15% payable on its first $50,000 in profit compared to the 28%, which I would have paid at that time as an individual or as a subchapter S corporation.

Most small businesses which initially incorporate will immediately make the subchapter S election to have the corporate profits flow directly through to their IRS 1040 tax return in order to avoid the "double taxation" issues of a corporation. Once my corporation had adequate working capital, I would pay myself an annual bonus at the end of the year so that the corporation had very little taxable income. I was required to pay a minimum taxable dividend to myself on the stock.

The characteristic of a corporation that makes it a popular business structure, is also what makes it a headache. As "corpus," the Latin root word for body would suggest, you have created a new body. This new "person" has a new set of special rules of operation and tax reports that will be required at all governmental levels. Even if it is a single bodied (owner) body, it is required to meet with itself once a year to pass resolutions and post them in its minute book. When it wants to open a business checking account or borrow money, the bank will require a formal signed "corporate resolution" to do so.

What NOT To Do

Why would anyone want to take a "simple" business like the sole proprietorship and turn it into a migraine headache? The fact is, nothing is simple when it comes to owning or managing a small business. Only the relative complexities of operating your business as a corporation allow me to use the word "simple" in referring to a proprietorship. I do not know the actual data, but I would venture to guess that most folks who establish their interests as a corporation, are basing their decision on the myth of "corporate immunity." S/he thinks, "If I borrow money to start my business and it fails, I will not lose my home to the bank." If you are a start-up business ... or even an existing business with a sudden need for capital ... you will *still* be required legally to "personally guarantee" the bank loan.

I know what you're thinking. "Well, if I have a huge uninsured loss or liability judgment made against my business, they will not be able to take my personal assets to satisfy the judgment." It is when something like this happens that business rookies get their first good schooling in the proper way to operate a sound corporation.

It is in court where you will learn, as a defendant, from the attorney representing the plaintiff what the phrase, "piercing the corporate veil" means. The short definition is it means, "We see right through you and you tried to cheat the system"— in other words, that you are "screwed" and will lose everything.

In day one of the trial you will learn that

incorporating your business gives you *no* protection.

It is ONLY when you incorporate and *carefully* operate your business *as* a corporation that you might have protection. This is how you show your "good faith."

Included in the first document request of the lawsuit will be your "minute" book. The attorney representing your antagonist is anxious to show the judge or jury that the last time your corporate officers met to satisfy the legal requirements for an annual meeting was four years ago. Then he will be happy to show the jury that when you opened a second bank account to receive credit card deposits, a copy of the required resolution was not signed, dated and inserted into your "minute" book.

To carry this hypothetical scenario further, the fun begins when the lawyer invites the jury to travel with you and your family to Disneyland, where he shows the jury that some travel expenses related to the vacation somehow got charged to your corporate credit card and you had forgotten to reimburse the corporation for these expenses. He will thus *prove* that you have No Integrity!

I could drivel on with many more examples, but hopefully I have made my point. Do not waste your time and money incorporating unless you plan to play by rather strict rules. One of the main rules is to **operate the corporation as a separate body**, even if you are the president, vice-president, and secretary-treasurer. Keep all transactions with yourself and with your other self at arm's length.

Stockholders

Another reason you might opt to incorporate is to divide ownership through the issuance of common stock *if there are going to be multiple owners*. If you do decide to incorporate, I suggest you read other publications to help you choose between a type C corporation, a type S corporation or, choosing to set up a limited liability company.

The most powerful document in the business world is undoubtedly **the partnership agreement**—it being the only one I know of that often **becomes a threat** to both your livelihood and your life itself. In its simplest form, a partnership agreement starts with two people who both wish to start a business, who agree to equally split both the investment costs and any profits gained from the business.

It would seem to make sense to join forces with someone who not only complements your skills, but also can double your start-up capital. The main problem with this type of arrangement is that eventually it will weaken your immune system and make you a candidate for illness and a shortened, miserable life.

For Instance

Somewhere out there, I am sure there is a partnership arrangement (although I am not aware of one) that has worked out for both partners. Let me tell you the outcomes of a couple that I *do* know about...

First, I will tell you about Harry, my printer. For at least twenty years Harry took care of all of my newsletter, stationary, and promotional printing needs. During the first ten years that I did business with him, I watched him become more and more miserable, because he was locked into a partnership with his brother-in-law. He hated working with a guy who started out okay but evolved into the ultimate jerk! How do you dump your wife's brother? Like divorce, such a break-up is very difficult. Thus, I say NEVER, NEVER, NEVER, NEVER, NEVER attach yourself to anyone in the form of a traditional two-person partnership venture. The chances for long-term failure approach 100%.

Eventually, Harry did start his own printing business, to get away from his toxic brother-in-law, and it was as if he had been reborn. I noticed a complete change in his facial expression and in his zest for life. He felt like a new man, enjoying his work because he was no longer overdosing on the cortisone released by his brain due to a very unhappy and stressful business relationship.

Sad to say, the damage of the partnership had been done. Harry died just a few years later of cancer. Now, I can't say that the early partnership caused his cancer, but I do know that it caused him ten years of stress and misery, so why take the chance? I suggest that all partnership agreements start with a bold disclaimer:

> **THE SURGEON GENERAL HAS DETERMINED THAT SIGNING THIS PARTNERSHIP AGREEMENT CAN BE HAZARDOUS TO YOUR HEALTH.**

Partnerships destroy partnerships. *Do not go into a business partnership with your spouse unless divorce is part of your long-term business plan.* I am not saying that a husband and wife should not collaborate in a business venture, but structure the business in one of the other forms that I am about to discuss.

I know of two brothers who will never speak to each other again. A wonderful relationship was plundered by their business partnership and the fallout has poisoned the whole family...

Bert and Ernie did all of the heating and cooling work for my stores. They also did work for the Procter and Gamble Company in Cincinnati, so they knew what they were doing when it came to HVAC issues. However, they didn't know Freon from foolishness when it came to starting and running a business. Bert and Ernie worked together in the field when I first met them with completely different styles. Bert was friendly and talkative, while Ernie worked on my air conditioner, giving an assist when needed. If Bert had come by himself he would have surely tried to talk my furnace into fixing itself. I saw less and less of Bert as he spent more time bidding jobs, and in doing office work, while Ernie came out with various helpers to get the work done.

I learned more about Bert and Ernie after the "divorce" and the company had dissolved. The trigger point in the collapse of the partnership and in the business was when Ernie bought a very expensive motor home. Bert had never made it out of the immobilized mobile home that he lived in when the business was started. They made a lot of money in the business. Bert enjoyed his spending it on a daily basis at the watering hole on the way home. Ernie saved his for the RV.

When Ernie bought the RV, Bert yelled foul, "I thought this was going to be an equal partnership. You have a new car, and now a new motor home and I have nothing. You screwed me, I quit."

Another risk in a small partnership is that
you are liable for the misdeeds of your partner.
If your partner runs off with all the money and leaves you with huge debts, you're stuck with them. Do not think that this cannot happen to you. I know of a case where it happened between "two BEST friends." Friend B was handling the financial aspects. Eventually the business started failing and friend A didn't even know it. Friend B vanished, leaving A with huge liabilities, including business payroll tax deductions that had been collected from employees but not deposited with the IRS.

If I had tried to figure out all of the rules of the IRS game I would have needed professional help from either a Ph.D. psychologist or an M.D. psychiatrist. Before you reach this point, may I suggest that you

get professional guidance from
both an attorney and a CPA.

They will be your most important business partners. Both of them are very likely to suggest that you form your new business as a Limited Liability COMPANY. I emphasize COMPANY since I often hear it mistakenly called a limited liability <u>corporation</u>. I suppose this happens because the acronym

LLC works just as well with the wrong name. The beauty of the LLC is that it provides you with advantages similar to the corporate structure without many of the hassles. Rather than creating a new body that has to go before the IRS for an annual autopsy, an LLC is invisible to federal taxing authorities. Instead, it is set up and governed under state law.

An LLC can have one or many owners. It is a very flexible organization governed by its operating agreement.

Chapter 2
SELECTING A MANAGER

Honesty has always served me well, so *"honestly"* I suggest that you DO NOT read this chapter unless you really are looking for a Store Manager. Compared to the other chapters, this one is long, boring, and pedantic. I have always been a big believer in recycling, and this is recycled and updated MBA work. The main reason I include it is to add bulk to the book. Honestly. I was told that if my book didn't contain at least one hundred pages, you would not buy it for the offered price.

On the other hand, this chapter could be useful to you, even if you worked with a cast of two! Even if you never need to hire a manager, you can use this chapter as a check up on yourself. Would you have hired "you" to manage the business if you had a choice? How do you rate yourself against the qualities and skills that I have identified and listed below? So if you feel inclined, read on for the many considerations in selecting an ideal store manager.

Customer Service

Customer service is the key to the success of the small independent business. This is the one area in which the smaller establishment can always outshine the larger chains if they so choose. To build your reputation and goodwill you must be willing to go the extra mile.

One can rightly conclude from this line of reasoning that a store manager must be highly *people oriented*. In other words, they should not be someone who concentrates on production (sales) at the expense of current customers. In competing against the major retailers, this factor can spell success or failure.

Word of mouth advertising will be your most potent weapon, and the success of this truth is directly dependent on the attention and courtesy given to customers. So, in selecting a retail store manager, you must attempt to choose someone who will be dedicated to serving the needs of the customer.

The Service of Selling

The job of a retail store is to sell. Other factors are not even relevant if there are not sufficient sales to sustain the store. Your manager must first be a "salesperson." Should you look for someone already trained in selling your type of merchandise? No! A salesperson is a salesperson is a salesperson. It doesn't matter whether they are selling stereos, lawn mowers, or plumbing services. It is much easier to teach someone about a product than it is to teach someone how to sell.

Some may argue that the idea of a "born sales person" has been overstated, that anyone can be taught the techniques of selling. That may be true, but in a small organization you cannot take the risk of trying to prove that point.

Look for someone who has been successful in sales of any sort. Their rapport skills can be easily transferred to your business. Prior experience with your products should be looked upon as a bonus, not as a criterion for selection.

A manager is supposed to manage, not primarily to sell. Why is it so important to choose a good salesperson to manage? Why not just look for a good manager? In some cases that might work, but if you hire a people-pleaser who is not also a salesperson, you might end up with lots of traffic but no sales.

The Passion of a Believer

A common characteristic of good managers is their ability to sell others on their ideas. For a retail store manager, this ability is essential. If a new product becomes available which the store will carry, the manager must be able to sell the subordinates on the product so that *they* will have the enthusiasm to sell the product to the customer. A store manager must be able to *sell his workers* on company policy and the necessity of first-rate customer service.

Being a good salesperson can be looked upon as a prerequisite to being a good manager. This is particularly true in a retail (selling) operation. In a small store, the manager often takes an active part in the sales end of the business, so the importance of hiring a first-rate sales person just cannot be over emphasized.

Some critical factors related to success in sales have been identified, and it would be worthwhile in hiring a manager to rate your applicants along these dimensions:

- Do they follow-up promptly on complaints, leads, orders, requests, etc?
- Do they plan ahead?
- Do they communicate effectively with others?
- Do they use new selling techniques?
- Are they persistent?

These are questions to keep in mind when you are contacting past employers and fellow employees for references.

It Pays to Be Organized

Hire someone who, in addition to selling, likes to plan, organize, coordinate, and delegate. These are the classic roles that define management. A manager who can delegate effectively will get more work done than one who tries to do all of the work himself. The manager should call the plays but let the subordinates run them. This will free up time for working on the long term goals of the business. Look for someone who has a superior level of intelligence and experience. This will be needed to command the respect of the other workers.

In hiring a retail store manager you will get in trouble if you are shortsighted and you merely seek someone who generates a lot of sales and cash. You must make sure that the manager has the "business sense" to hang on to the cash generated. If the manager concentrates too heavily on herding sales in the front door, the profit may be leaving through the back door. It is just as important to control expenses as it is to generate sales. The manager you hire must have a keen understanding of the difference between gross profit and net profit. If not, it is unlikely there will be any of the second.

If your store is to succeed your manager will need the determination, ability, and "guts" to run a tight ship. The manager will have to hold the profit margin in the face of what appears to be severe price competition.

Jack of All Trades

The manager of a small business has to be "universal" in abilities. In addition to selling and managing, the person will at least have to know the basics in the following areas:

Accounting—He or she must be able to understand the meaning of the store's balance sheet and income statement. Studying them will point out necessary remedial action that the business needs to make. These statements will also suggest steps that can be taken to increase profitability.

Advertising—The manager needs to know the difference between true advertising and donations to non-profit organizations, and how to make a good advertising buy.

Personnel—The manager should have the major role in selecting the subordinates, and know the appropriate procedure to follow in hiring.

Psychology—The manager will have to know how people think. He or she must know how to motivate the sales force to sell, and know how to help motivate the customer to buy.

To find a person who is an expert in all of these areas you could look forever. The idea to keep in mind is that they are all relevant to your business. Choose the person who is the best qualified overall.

Qualifications to Serve

In order to be able to fill the multiple roles of a retail store manager, some general qualifications should be mandatory. A high school degree, and a number of years' business experience would probably be the minimum if your manager is really going to be the one "who calls the shots." It is more likely that candidate you choose to hire will have a college degree.

The only way that you will be able to continue to open additional stores is to hire people competent enough to successfully operate the stores with as little dependence as possible on you. If you cannot feel at ease delegating the entire operation to the manager, then you have the wrong person as your manager. This does not mean that you divorce yourself completely from the branch store. A total lack of supervision is a sure road to disaster. You must hire someone capable of running the day-to-day operations with your overall supervision as opposed to your active participation.

Previous experience with a large company in the retail arena could be a big asset to your organization. The new manager may very well bring with him a wealth of proven marketing and management techniques. This experience could easily prove to be much more valuable than a formal education. They will know techniques that have worked successfully in the "real" world.

If your candidate has worked for a competitor, the amount of new training required would be minimized. Knowing how your competitor operates can give you a big advantage in competing effectively. As stated earlier, experience with a competitor should be looked upon as a bonus rather than a prerequisite to hiring.

A hazard of hiring someone who has worked for a competitor is that after the first week, you will have an employee who knows much more than you do. Policies and procedures from the previous work place will come along, and the only way to extinguish the unwanted ones will be to extricate your rival's business from your own, without burning the house down, at once! Be careful!

History Lessons

The main advantage of past experience is that you will have an indication of the candidate's abilities. Studying their past performance should clue you in as to whether or not they will be able to live up to your expectations. The best indicator of future success is past success, so look for someone with a successful business or sales record.

In a separate chapter I mentioned *location, location, **location*** as being vital to the success of a small business. When it comes to choosing all personnel, it is *personality, personality, **personality.*** The manager and team that you hire will represent your organization to the public. If you hire a successful "salesperson" type manager you will almost automatically hire someone with a pleasant, likeable personality. Along with personality, you will want to examine the person's appearance, dress, and mannerisms. This is one area in which the interview can be used effectively. It will give you the opportunity to observe all of these characteristics first hand. As mentioned before, because of the nature of the retail business, the manager must be strongly oriented to serving the needs of the customer.

Warning! Do not hire someone who used a typewriter or a computer to complete the job application form. They may not write legibly. Insist on a sample of their handwriting. I have had mechanics who scrawled amounts on service invoices. Every nine that looked like a two cost me seven or seventy bucks.

Since your manager is to be "the boss" you should seek someone who is "self-motivating." Many people in the sales business are of this type. Theoretically, you want a manager who will work as hard at managing your store as they would if it were their own store. How close you can come to this ideal will depend partly on the program you have to offer, as explained elsewhere in this book, and partly on the person you choose.

During the interview you should seek answers to the following questions:

1) How many hours a week are you scheduled to work at your current job?
2) How many hours do you normally work?
3) Is working overtime a hassle?
4) If married, how does your spouse feel about you working long hours?

Of course, the answers to these questions are best obtained through a larger number of much subtler and less direct questions.

A store manager will not succeed if he/she thinks he/she can work 9 to 5, five days a week. Some evening and weekend hours will be a necessity. The trend toward Sunday sales is stronger than ever today. You may be required to be open by your lease, or need to open for competitive reasons. In many instances the manager will get "stuck" working these longer hours. Try to hire someone who is highly motivated by the nature of the work itself. This way, the less extrinsic motivation and reward (money) you will have to provide. Structure the job to have appeal. Let the manager truly "be their own boss" as much as possible. Many people value freedom over money. If you structure the job properly and fill it with the right person you can get "more" for "less".

In considering a married person it would be ideal if you could "interview" the spouse. You will be in direct competition with them for the employee's time. The less tolerant they are of your manager working long hours, the less time the manager is likely to devote to the operation of the business. It might be wise to treat the prospect and their spouse to dinner. This would give you the opportunity to do your spouse "interview".

CHARACTER

This should be investigated as thoroughly as possible. If you have less than 100% confidence in the honesty and integrity of the applicant, you would do well to move on to the next one. I have seen many businesses go under because of mistakes made here.

To continue to grow your business, you need people to whom you can delegate as much control as possible with a minimum amount of supervision. No matter how effectively you watch, do not for a moment think you can keep a dishonest person honest. It is virtually impossible to keep a determined thief from "shaking you down". This sad fact of life led to a bar-owner friend of mine having a policy of hiring bartenders with the understanding of, *"I am going to pay you ten dollars per hour and I know a good bartender can easily steal two bucks an hour, so you will make twelve until you get caught, and then you are fired."*

My counsel for you is to hire honest people, treat them fairly and generously, and build into your business the best possible system of checks and balances so your employees are not motivated or tempted to cheat.

Although honesty is probably the most important characteristic, it is also one of the most difficult ones to measure or determine. It is an area that requires an intuitive judgment. Personal references or character references will aid in making the correct judgment. A certain amount of credibility should be subtracted to compensate for the "halo effect". Anything less than a perfect character reference should be considered suspect.

Because of the "let's sue" mentality of our culture, business-savvy

17

prior employers will not give out references. To be perfectly safe you should never give out anything other than "name, rank, and serial number" for people that have worked for you. That is, when they started, when they quit, what their duties were, and wage level if you wish to share it. Until we solve the lawyer glut problem in this country, you will have to operate your business with your hands tied.

Not everyone is aware of the potential liabilities, so try to find out as much as you can. Phone calls should be made to the past and current employers. Fellow employees and other acquaintances of the applicants should also be contacted. Calls or personal visits are superior to written requests for information. Most individuals will be more candid and open if their statements are not in writing. Ask for four references and do not even bother calling the one listed first. Start at the bottom and work your way up through number two. The first one listed was chosen for their positive bias.

A retail credit check will often reveal information helpful in determining the overall financial and personal stability of the applicant. Watch for "red flags." A history of job, personal, or financial problems should be avoided like the plague. Trust me, there are enough problems in managing a retail business; you won't need to import any.

If you have a candidate who qualifies in every way except integrity, you have a candidate who will make a lot of money — for himself!

The Spider and the Fly

The key to successful hiring is aggressive recruiting. In order to attract a sufficient pool of applicants, the position offered must be enticing. Once you have decided what qualifications you would like to have in your Store Manager, you will need a "darn good" program to convince the candidate to accept your offer. As a rule, the small company will fall short if it tries to compete with the benefits offered by the large corporations. Since you cannot match them on these points, you have to offer the candidate something else that will be equally enticing.

As mentioned earlier, the "be your own boss" is an old but successful appeal. You have to set up your branch store operation so that the manager is truly "their own boss". If the manager gets a good "share of the action," they will not only be attracted to the job, but they will be highly motivated once on the job. A good bonus or profit-sharing system is a must, not only in attracting new personnel, but also in keeping your current people.

Good health and pension plans are available through many insurance companies for the small business. A new employee will probably be looking for one of these plans. Health benefits are a killer cost for the small business owner. Give fifty extra points to any applicants who come fully covered by the spouse's job! If you don't have to provide health care insurance, you can make the wage look much more attractive.

The larger the number of prospective managers you have to choose from, the greater the chance that you will find a highly qualified candidate. Think about this next time you have fresh lobster at the Red Lobster. Who is more likely to find the ideal lobster for dinner? Someone who picks from a tank with six live lobsters or sixty? I say: double the size of the pool of applicants you choose from and double your probability of success. Be aggressive in advertising and promoting the position. If you were to hire an employee for $50,000 per year, you might hope for at least a ten-year relationship. You need to think of your selection as a half a million-dollar purchase, because that is exactly what it is. Put just as much effort and energy and intelligence in choosing your employee as you would a $500,000.00 home or other piece of real estate.

Before starting your recruiting, it is important to start with a profile of the person you are seeking, and a job description. This will limit the number of places that you will have to look. One place to find a retail store manager is in a retail store. By keeping your eyes and ears open you can learn of potential candidates. It would be a good idea to maintain an up-to-date list of "Possibilities" for all positions in your business. Even if there is no immediate need, keeping a list like this can be a real blessing when the need arises. When the competitive grapevine brings you a "success" story, it would pay to make some notes for future reference. A list like this is the perfect place to start when the time comes that you must find a store manager. Even if a choice is not possible from the list, it would serve as a good basis to do some comparative shopping. Whenever I meet a particularly nice manager at a store like Radio Shack, I always ask for his or her business card.

An Employment Agency

If you choose to engage their services, a professional employment agency will suggest a number of candidates. For the small business, they can provide a number of services which would not be available within the organization. They can do all the recruiting, pre-screening, interviewing, and testing. In a sense, the small employer can "rent" an employment department similar to the ones which large corporations have in house.

The employer is smart to choose an agency where *he* has to pay the fee. He will have a much better group of candidates provided for him. A truly qualified candidate should be in such demand that he will not have to pay someone to find him a job. He or she will be in a position to have someone pay to find them. Exceptional people generally have job offers find them. They seldom have to hunt.

The best candidates are not looking for work.
They *have* work. Seek, and you shall find them.

Don't forget that the employment agency is in business for profit. They make a profit by placing as many people as possible as quickly as they can, just as you do when you turn your inventory quickly. Don't be surprised if they build up each suggested candidate and say they are the perfect one for you. To make a sale, they have to "sell" you on the credentials of the person they have in mind for you. A reliable agency will suggest only good people to you, but you must be cautious to either select the one who you feel is the best, or be willing to reject all of their suggestions and shop elsewhere, or go back to a source of your own.

Most agencies will charge you around 10% of the new employee's first year's salary. If, through their service, you obtain someone who is 10%

more productive, you will break even the first year, and are ahead for every following year that the person works for you.

Other sources of candidates are: the unemployment bureau, newspaper classified ads, college placement offices, your customer list, small "Help Wanted" ads placed within one of your display ads, a notice on your marquee, and internet sites like monster.com. Think creatively. Remember, you want as many qualified applicants as you can possibly attract.

The state employment office will put you in touch with people who need jobs. It would pay to screen these applicants extra carefully. Since you are not paying a fee, you shouldn't expect to find many highly qualified candidates in this manner. A newspaper ad will put you in touch with some good applicants as long as you specify in your ad the minimum qualifications that you will accept.

Since a small business does not have the training abilities of a large company, it is unlikely that you would want to hire a recent college graduate. It would be better to look for someone who is "trained" and who has a successful business track record. Besides, you would have a difficult time competing with the "big name" companies for the better graduates. Give the graduate a few years to get trained by the large corporation, and also get sick of its policies and politics, so that they are ripe to take their experience elsewhere, and enjoy the advantages of working in a small, warm, loving environment.

The Interview

Specific instances where the interview can be used as a valuable screening and selection tool are mentioned in this section.

There are some general rules that should be followed in interviewing.
1) Don't waste your time asking questions about items that can be obtained from the resume or application

2) If you structure your interview, it will be more reliable

3) Do not use leading questions

4) Evaluate the applicant along specific dimensions in the interview

5) Be careful not to form your impressions too early in the interview, since this is a common tendency and pitfall

6) Use this opportunity to sell yourself but be careful not to dominate the interview

Even though only limited validity has been demonstrated for the personal interview, it is probably one of the better tools available to small business owners. There are not a lot of viable alternatives, so use it to your fullest advantage. The small business person, accustomed to making intuitive judgments and decisions, should feel quite comfortable using the interview.

It is unlikely that you, as a small businessperson, will be in a position to comprehensively test your candidates. As mentioned earlier, this can be done by an employment agency if you engage their services. A private business or industrial psychologist could be hired to administer tests to the more promising applicants. It is questionable whether the information gained would be useful enough to justify the costs. Most of the information that you need can be obtained through a thorough check of the candidate's job experience record.

A feeling for the candidate's level of intelligence can normally be obtained from the interview. Close attention to the applicant's diction will be a good clue. I personally look for people with bright eyes who wear a smile. I swear I can measure a person's IQ to within ten points by looking deeply into their eyes for a sparkle. Although these are not scientific methods, they serve as a practical and reasonable alternative to a more precise determination.

A simple test you can devise yourself is the "in basket" test. This test is quite simple to administer and should give you a lot of good data if devised to closely simulate the situations that would normally be encountered in the job of the manager. Some suggestions for test items would be:

1) to answer a letter from an irate customer; we've all had a few "customers from hell" so you ought to be able to find a real letter which needed a courteous response in spite of the source
2) to choose a TV commercial schedule from three or four choices
3) to make financial or other management recommendations from a sample balance sheet and income statement
4) to make a sales presentation for any real or fictitious product.

An even simpler test could be a "verbal" in-basket test. In an interview you could ask the applicant:
1) How would you handle this situation?
2) What would you do if this happened?
3) What would you do and say if an employee did this?
An in-basket test gives you the opportunity to observe first hand how the prospective employee reacts to job-like situations and problems.

Government agencies have been established to insure that selection tests will not be discriminatory. You need to be sure that your test is both reliable and valid. That is, will the test give the same answer consistently when applied to the same group of people, and does the performance on the test accurately predict on-the-job performance? If using a bought test, make sure that these two characteristics have been demonstrated for it.

Some personnel professionals have suggested using biographical information as an alternative to testing. This concept is based on the premise that "past behavior predicts future behavior." Items like a person's rank in the military, courses taken in school, club memberships in school, etc. have been used successfully to predict job performance. Basically, you are looking for a pattern that demonstrates motivation and achievement. This approach cannot really substitute for testing, and I believe it should be thought of as a supplement rather than an alternative.

In any small product or service business, the largest single expense is Salaries/Commissions. A mistake in the selection of personnel could destroy the chance of success. If you are a small organization with only one store, and are adding a second, you will be choosing fifty percent of your managerial staff. The success of the new locations will be more dependent on your manager's abilities than any other factor, by far, other than perhaps, location. The store manager will be the "captain of the team," the "key" man or woman as dubbed by the insurance companies that offer policies to protect the loss of such a critical asset. It would be difficult to devote too much time or expense in seeking and selecting this "key" person.

Get Ready, Get Set, HIRE!

How do you actually go about making the decision? Unfortunately there is no magic formula for making this job easy! There is no secret or sure-fire way of knowing if you are making the correct selection. The most commonly suggested approach to take is known as the "total assessment system". Rather than narrowing the applicants down through a "hurdles" approach, you hold your decision on the potential candidates until you have developed a well-rounded picture of each one. You look carefully at each of the many different points outlined here, cross your fingers, and decide. I have found that this recommended approach left me in a state of near perpetual confusion and conflict. I tend to feel "fogged out" with the "total assessment system."

Once I have a small pool of applicants, maybe a fourth of the total I expect to screen, I'll pick the best from that group, generally using a scored rating system to make the comparison as objective as possible. I then use this applicant as the measure by which to compare all new applicants, never again having to consider more than two at a time, always keeping the best of any comparison. If your goal was to determine the largest leaf in your yard, this is really the only way you could do it without going crazy. Use the methods that work best for you. Remember, you are the expert at your business! Be confident! Following these steps, you will have done your homework and should have success.

However, mistakes happen and people change. If you need to terminate a manager (or any employee), do it sooner rather than later. In today's litigious society, always seek legal council BEFORE you make the cut, as it is likely to be nasty and could cost you dearly even if no laws are broken. The goal is not only to obey all employment laws, but also to minimize any chance of false claims being filed against you, which can literally cost thousands of dollars to have dismissed in a court of law. Pay close attention to the specific situation I will discuss in the chapter on general personnel issues.

If I had read a book like this early in my business career, I might have saved myself over $120,000.00 in attorney's fees. That story is a book in itself ... yet to be published.

Chapter 3
SELECTING YOUR LOCATION

A classic business theorem in the lodging industry is that the three most important factors for the success of a motel or hotel are
location,

        location,

                and **location.**

Most small businesses, particularly retailers, should adopt this theorem for their own success.

I inherited a less than ideal location when I took over my Dad's business. I stuck with it, though, since shortly after taking over the business, I decided to buy the building — a decision that probably cost me *severely* in lost sales over the years. But when I opened my second store, carefully *researching the location* as the thesis for my Master's Degree in marketing, it was ***destined* for success**. It was not long before sales at the new location exceeded those at the first.

Over time, the original location fell further and further behind. At least 80% of the reason for this paradigm shift related to the factors I had considered in choosing the ideal location for store number two. Demographics!

The demographics (including age, population growth, discretionary income and family structure) were 200% better! Highway access and parking was also twice as good. Foot traffic, and having compatible business neighbors, helped the new business.

I am convinced that poor location decisions contribute most heavily to the many small business failures occurring each year in the United States. Many other businesses survive, but do not achieve the high level of success they could with a better location. Perhaps they do not realize that cheap rent is no bargain. A poor location can cost a business lost sales and profits far exceeding the amount saved each month in lower rental payments.

Many people think that choosing a store location is something you do only when opening a new store or relocating an existing one. Actually, you make a location decision every year when you consciously or unconsciously decide to stay put. It is too easy to get settled into a less than ideal position. You should use the procedure outlined below to evaluate your current location against all existing alternatives each and every year. Ask yourself, "Where would I locate my business if I were just starting it?" That is the place you should probably consider moving to. Consider the cost to move an investment that will pay tremendous dividends for years and years.

Identify Your Customer Base

The first step in considering demographic factors is to recognize that every product or service appeals primarily to a distinctive class of people. The importance of knowing the profile of your typical customer cannot be overstated. Almost every consumer product company asks demographic questions on their warranty cards. This data, which should be available from your manufacturer or distributor, is essential in planning a business location. If you are a professional service provider, check with your industry's trade association for this data.

You want to know your typical customer's age, income level, family size, and gender. The next step is to analyze your market area to find the areas where your "typical" customer is most likely to reside.

You should plot the average age of the people in your market area on a map. You may wish to let different colors represent various age brackets of the population. After your map is completed it will be easy to see which areas have the highest concentrations of families most likely to patronize your business. Do the same for income. The reason for wanting to know the location of the higher income areas is obvious.

A similar procedure should be followed for population density, and population growth. Population growth should be looked at because it is just as important to know where the people are moving as it is to know where they are living! Which areas are growing, and which areas are declining? Reminds me of the famous hockey player who described his reason for being a super star as "skating to where the puck was headed rather than where it was at."

Population density is of lesser importance than the study of age, income, and growth. The main consideration is not to locate "too far" out from the center of a city. "Too far" is where the population becomes so sparse that your trading area would not permit your business to thrive.

Most of the older and larger metropolitan areas follow a similar pattern. As you move out from the center of the city average age will decrease, income will increase, and population growth will increase. This is the reason almost all of your new retail businesses are found in the suburban areas. The four factors discussed above must be considered jointly when choosing the best location for your frame shop, coffee shop, or dental practice.

Make Them Feel at Home

Once you know the area where you wish to locate, depending on the type of business, a major decision could be **whether to locate in an established shopping center, or mall, or go it alone in a free standing location.**

In opening a new store location you have three major choices:

1) You can seek admission to a planned shopping center or mall.

2) You can locate in an established (though unplanned) suburban business strip center.

3) You can develop a store with its own parking facilities on or off a traffic artery.

Planned shopping centers can be divided into two types:

(1)   A "*convenience* center" will carry such items as groceries, drugs, hardware, liquor, and usually some variety and service stores. You may even find a small apparel or shoe store in the convenience good center, but the large majority of the tenants will be of the type mentioned above.

(2) By contrast, a "*goods* center" will usually have apparel, appliances, jewelry, furniture, and similar items that can be distinguished by their relatively infrequent purchase and higher price. They are so named because customers engage in "shopping" for quality, price, and style. This type of center will almost always also contain a number of the convenience stores, but those will be of secondary importance.

A planned center has the big advantage of built-in "guaranteed" traffic. Also, because they are "planned", you can be protected from directly competing merchants. However, these same centers give preference in rentals and entry permits to the big chain stores. You might not be able to get in, and if you could the terms might be so unattractive as to change your mind about desiring entry.

Many small stores, which have established a branch or relocated in a planned center, have not done well in spite of the traffic attracted to the center. Besides the problem with the high rent, trouble can develop because of the difference in character of the shopping center and the shop itself. A shopping center is ideal for stores that cater to mass demand—the big department store, the popular price specialty store, the variety store, and the supermarket. It is not as ideal for smaller independent stores.

When you move or open an additional store in a shopping center, your customers might not follow you to your new location. The mass of shoppers at the center may not really do you that much good—not when you consider what you will be paying to have them there.

The String Street Location

You might be able to do almost as much business with a lot less overhead in a "string street location" which is a site on or just off a major highway. You can usually provide your own parking facilities at moderate cost. This type of location is normally ideal for the small or medium size store selling goods of high unit value of special interest to the suburbanite. You could not expect much of the impulse buying, which occurs in a planned center, but those who drove in would be there to buy.

The primary consideration in such an isolated location should be parking and general accessibility. It should be a known location that most of the people in your market area are familiar with. It should be relatively easy to get to from all directions.

A store that generates its own traffic can do well in a string street location, unlike the greeting card shop, which needs to feed from pedestrian traffic, or the restaurant, which must feed from either pedestrian or motor traffic. The rent savings in an isolated location can allow you to advertise, in order to create your own traffic. In fact, you can think of advertising and rent as reciprocals. You will only have so much money in your budget to spend on these two items. You can spend almost all of it on rent in a planned shopping center, or you can spend almost all of it on advertising in an independent location.

The best location for a business that wants to draw from a relatively large trading area is where a major radial highway leading from downtown intercepts a major circumferential highway. Other things being equal, the site should be on the right hand side coming from downtown. As far as possible the site should be prominent and easily visible. A high volume of traffic is not important or even desirable. It is the accessibility and familiarity of the location that are important.

All of us have had residential neighbors that have been a joy and some that have caused misery to point that we were tempted to move. The same is true with business neighbors. Part of the reason for the demise of the third store I opened was the mistake of opening in a brand new strip center with several spots yet to be leased. I did not follow my own advice in choosing this strip center. The developer got desperate for tenants and I ended up being two doors from the "Hong Kong Health Spa" and just a few more doors from the "Circus", a teen nightclub. Prostitution and drunks were not compatible neighbors for a sewing machine business, which catered to a female clientele.

Once you begin to look for a specific store in the location you have chosen, you must take a close look at who your neighbors will be. Will they hurt your business, help it, or have no effect? That is, how compatible will they be? A high **degree of compatibility** exists between two businesses which, because of their adjacency, do more volume together than they would if separated. This high compatibility may come about because the businesses are complementary in nature or because, though competitive, they carry goods of different styles, lines and prices, thereby increasing total patronage through cumulative attraction in locations that have a trade area adequate to support two stores. The measure of compatibility is the degree to which the two businesses interchange customers. The more interchange of customers between the two stores the more total business each will do. Also, businesses of similar size will generate more additional sales than if one is large relative to the other.

Automobile dealers have realized the benefit of clustering. Near my Cincinnati home, Kings Auto Mall allows a customer shopping for a new vehicle to see almost every brand. Shoe stores knew it long ago. It was not uncommon to find an intersection in a downtown shopping area with all four corners of an intersection occupied by shoe stores.

In choosing a location, you want to focus on the positive aspects that will enhance and support your business. However, you must be aware of possible negatives. Pedestrian interruptions work against customer interchange; consequently, they are highly incompatible neighbors. Some of the most common interruptions are vacant buildings, driveways, cross traffic (auto or pedestrian), as well as hazardous, noisy, or otherwise unpleasant detractions.

The success of the large shopping centers has resulted from careful application of the above principles. You should give it the same attention when choosing the location for your store.

Parking

Do not fail to consider the impact of easy access and adequate parking on the success of your business. Parking should be available as close as possible to the store entrance. The parking lot must be visible from the street. It is more important that the parking lot be visible than that the store be visible. People will soon learn that your store is there, but they will not come in unless they know they have a place to park. Rear parking is to be avoided at almost any cost. Its only value will be to provide a place for the employee's cars and it will have some value during seasonal sales peaks when front parking is overloaded.

Not to sound sexist but women drivers particularly dislike going "around in back" without knowing just how difficult the maneuvering required will be and whether there is, in fact, a parking space available at all. One shopping center in the Chicago area has two parking lots, one in front and the other in back, of about the same size. On peak shopping days there are shoppers cruising around and around the front lot looking for a space while the back lot is half empty. The shopping center is twenty-five years old, and most of the people who shop there have been coming to it for years. The back lot has never been filled, and the front lot is full to capacity even on average weekdays.

You should, to the best of your ability, determine the amount of parking that you need and provide that amount <u>and no more</u>. Space should be provided to accommodate all of your customers during your weekly sales peaks. You should not try to provide for seasonal peaks. During peak season it is better to let some customer's park outside the lot in an overflow lot than to have extra spaces that will be unused the rest of the year. If you have "too much" parking, the large bare lot will make your store appear unsuccessful and unattractive. People are very strongly attracted by congestion. Congestion creates an atmosphere of excitement. People are repelled by congestion only when it becomes seriously uncomfortable or disadvantageous to them.

People Attract People

As a small business consultant and advocate of small business owners, I often stop in a small independently owned restaurant with a near empty parking lot and tell them to move their employee cars into the front lot to make the food more appealing. People follow people like sheep. An empty lot is the worst possible advertising.

Years ago, at Al Hirt's place on Bourbon Street in New Orleans, the doorman always kept a line of people waiting to get in no matter how many empty tables were inside. Al knew how to blow his horn in more ways than one.

The benefits of a nice parking area can be seriously compromised by poor access. A lot is preferred which has a safe easy turn in and out from or to either direction of the highway. A traffic light at or near the entrance is often times an advantage.

One final item ought to be considered concerning the parking lot. Can it be expanded? As your sales grow and you become established, your space requirements may increase. Failure to plan far into the future might create a costly handicap later on.

Having considered everything we discussed, do you think you're done? Think again.

Lease or Purchase

Will you lease or will you buy a business location? It is impossible to say whether leasing or buying is better for the average businessperson, since each method has its inherent advantages and disadvantages. For instance:

You should probably lease space if:

1) you are, or plan to be, growing rapidly with increasing space needs;

2) you do not have a large cash surplus. Opening a new location will increase your inventory and accounts receivable requirements. You must be careful not to have your growth stunted because the money you need for working capital is tied up in a building;

3) you do not wish to take the risk of loss which might result from declining property values; and

4) you plan to occupy the building for a relatively short period of time.

You might consider buying the property if:

1) you wish to have your occupancy rights guaranteed for an unusually long term;

2) you can purchase the building without straining your liquidity and wish to have equity in a fixed asset. Having the building as collateral for a bank loan could be a life saver for the business if a temporary financial problem develops or if funds are needed for expansion;

3) you can afford to provide the necessary maintenance and repairs to the building as it ages; and/or

4) the property will be fairly easy to sell in the future, if this action becomes necessary.

Since each alternative has its advantages, you should not get stuck on one and limit your location possibilities as a result. You may wish to buy property, but in many cases the owner may not wish to sell because of tax or other financial considerations. In this situation the owner will make the lease terms a lot more attractive than he would an outright purchase. If this is the best location for you, take it and forget about buying the property. Whether you leasing or buy is a secondary concern to finding the optimal location.

The Agreement

Once you have a found a place to lease, it is imperative to

negotiate a favorable agreement. Because of all the variations, this can be almost as tricky as choosing your location. There are three basic types of agreements:

1) "the flat amount lease" involves a fixed monthly charge independent of sales volume. This is a very favorable arrangement if your sales are fairly stable month to month;

2) "the straight percentage" lease, which permits the rent to fluctuate with either sales volume or profits. This arrangement makes the property owner a "partner" in your business; the owner shares some of the risk and expects a greater return for doing so. In an area where the property value will be increasing because of favorable population shifts, the owner might insist on this type of arrangement so that he may share in the benefits; and

3) the "percentage lease with a minimum guarantee" is a slight variation of the above. This is to protect the lesser against a sharp decline in sales. Usually the minimum is quite a bit less than what would be encountered in the "flat-amount" lease.

There is a wide range of percentages which one might expect to pay. One must consider the probable sales per square foot; the degree which the tenant generates the business as against the degree to which the location generates it; the gross margin on the products to be sold; and, the probability of reaching and maintaining the anticipated sales volume in establishing a fair rate to pay.

Don't overlook the possibility of a lease with an option to buy. This might give you the best of both worlds.

If you do favor purchasing property, then you should consider ownership and sub rental. This is an arrangement whereby you construct or purchase a building larger than you need and rent a portion of it. The rental will help pay for part of the cost of carrying the building itself, and thus reduce the owner's overhead on his business. Such an arrangement is often times more financially sound and easier to amortize than a single store unit.

The drawback to this arrangement is that it requires more capital, added financing and interest costs, as well as the risk of having a vacant portion of the building.

Second Site

If you intend to open a second business location in the same city as the first, it would be helpful to know where your current customers are located. That is, what is your current trading area? Every marketing expert has a slightly different definition of trade area. The most simple is, "the geographic area from which a business draws the majority of its customers". Sears identifies their "primary trading area" as the region in which 75% of the store's credit customers reside, and a "secondary trading area" as the region that provides the next 15% of the store's customers. For most retail stores the primary trade area is a radius around the store extending two to five miles.

How can you determine the trading area of your store? You could sponsor a contest and plot the address of the entries on a map. A simpler yet more valuable procedure would be to plot the addresses from your sales invoices. If your store is located in a city with a number of zip code areas, then you can easily compute the percentage of customers for each zip code. The area that contains two- thirds to three-fourths of your customers is your primary trade area.

Most likely you will be amazed at how heavily your sales are concentrated in the area closest to your store. Products with the smallest trade area tend to be low in cost, consumed frequently, and available many places. Exclusive and expensive products will have a much larger trade area. In other words there are more places to buy milk or bread than Rolls Royce automobiles.

The above information will show you how far from the current location the second one should be. If it is too close you will be competing for your own customers. If you locate in an area that accounts for only 10 to 15% of your current business, you will draw most business away from your competitors and not yourself.

Competition

Speaking of competition, before choosing your first or additional store locations, it is useful to know the location of all competitive stores. Plotting them on a map will make it easy to pin point those areas that are least adequately served. Depending on your type of business you may want to be close to or far away from the competition. If your merchandise is superior to the competitors, and the competitor promotes heavily you might benefit from the traffic which they draw by being near by. If you lack the "guts" you can try to get away from the competition and try to carve out your own little market area. You can never be sure, however, that a competitor will not move close to you.

Try to position your business between the current competition and the largest area of un-served population. People will rarely go through a business district or pass by a shopping center to get the same product further on.

The research and analysis behind choosing a store location is really quite easy. *Making the decision is the hard part!* It is difficult to make the decision because of so many factors to consider. Each location will have its favorable and unfavorable characteristics. It is a matter of weighing the good points against the bad points for each possible site. It is difficult mentally because it is probably the most important business decision that you will ever make. You will be risking all the capital and energy that you put into the new venture.

Because the location decision is so complex and so critical, the procedure outlined in this chapter must not be skipped. All of the factors discussed must be examined and studied carefully. If you compromise and settle for an inferior location you will be paying for it in lost sales and profits as long as you operate there. You will have saved nothing and there is no way to measure the extent of your great loss.

Even if you do everything as precisely as you should, you might still choose a less than optimal location. You cannot foretell all of the changing variables. No one can predict the exact future of the location, what your competitors will do, what your best future product line will be, the number of additional stores you may wish to open, what your future sales and cash flow will be, etc. At least the analysis will have minimized your chances for error. You will have made an error of judgment which is usually a lot less damaging than a bad guess.

To recap, you should choose the general area for the store **first** by synthesizing all of the information that you have collected on age, income, density, and growth of the population along with you knowledge of the location of competition and current and proposed highways. The **next** step is to choose the optimal site within the optimal area. You may wish to pick out four or five alternate sites and rate them with some type of a scoring chart for parking, access, traffic, visibility, and compatibility of neighboring businesses. You should **then** decide on a first, second, and third choice since your choices may be limited by the lease terms available.

Once you have begun your new operation you should give the business two or three years to develop. If the operation has not met your expectations and it seems that location rather than poor management is at fault, it is time to start looking all over again for a place to move. Hopefully, you haven't gotten yourself into an unbearable lease so that this option to move will be available to you.

If you are opening a properly positioned second store, sales at the first store should ultimately increase because of two factors: 1) prospective buyers will have more confidence in the long range stability of a business with two, rather than one location 2) the second location will permit a larger promotional budget because of the great reduction of waste circulation that currently exists when advertising in any of the major media. In fact, more efficient advertising is one of the primary benefits that would be realized by opening additional locations.

The specific site selected should provide adequate parking with easy access to or from either direction of the highway. A three of five year renewable, flat rate lease would be ideal. Compatible neighbors all around would be terrific.

The Endless Quest

How long should you plan to look for this "ideal" location? Forever, because it does not exist! You must be satisfied by locating your store on a site that approaches the ideal *as closely as possible.*

You can get assistance in choosing a site and securing data from a number of sources. Your gas, electric, or telephone utility may have a person designated to help you in making the location decision. Some banks and insurance companies also provide such a service. A real estate agent who specializes in commercial sales can be helpful. His recommendations are likely to be influenced by his interest in the commission from making a sale or lease, so do not accept his advice as the final word. Your local Chamber of Commerce and the Small Business Administration are usually very willing and able to help you.

Generally there is no charge for the services of the above groups, so it is foolish not to call upon them for assistance. If you feel you need more help, you might consider hiring a professional consultant who specializes in the field. Remember the decision you do make can literally assure your success, or doom you to failure.

Chapter 4

BANKERS: BUDDIES OR BAD GUYS?

Do you need a loan?

Do not go to your banker.

Go to your *neighbor's* banker!

When I needed a loan, the bank I had supported for years with my checking account and credit card deposits was the least friendly. Every time I borrowed money to support the growth of my business, I was forced to establish a new business relationship with a new bank.

You would think that someone to whom you had given all of your banking business would be your friend. The traditional assumption is that a business owner should have an established relationship with his banker, in the event he ever needs to borrow money. The mentality of the bankers that I had worked with, however, seemed to be that if you had been a long-term loyal customer, they had earned the right to make you suffer through a long-term painful loan application process. They might ultimately offer you a loan with painful rates and terms, but my advice is, if you need a loan, go to a bank who *wants* your business, not one who *has* your business.

Shopping for Money

In the late 1970's, inflation was wild. With prices soaring, some times I would be selling machines that I had purchased at two price notches lower than current prices, greatly increasing my gross margin. And as a sewing machine wholesale distributor, as well as a large retailer, I could make significant "inventory profits" by stocking up on merchandise.

My father and I had dealt with Central Trust Bank for years. I guess I was naïve, thinking I could borrow money from the bank across the street where our business had been depositing money for the last fifteen years. I went to the bank manager and told him of my opportunity to increase my profits by stocking up on merchandise. He didn't deny me a loan; it was more like he seized it as an opportunity to initiate a sadistic torture ritual. Upon request, I submitted about three and three-quarter pounds of paper to fulfill the application requirements. I provided evidence of our complete credit worthiness showing a solid financial history going back many years.

My reward was their offer of an installment loan requiring a lien on the inventory that I wanted to purchase. The installment loan carried a particularly onerous annual percentage rate. The requirements related to the lien were just as onerous. This was a double slap in my face, since the rate was ridiculously high, and I did not see the need to track serial numbers for the bank. The bottom line was that this bank, which we had supported for many years with our business, was being a very bad business buddy. I said, "No, thank you," and "good-bye."

About a week later I was having lunch with my attorney, Mr. Jack Stith, discussing other issues, when I just happened to mention my frustrated attempts at securing my first bank loan. My attorney referred me to his friend, Mr. Gene Gaines, a commercial loan officer with National City Bank. (The names of the banks have changed over the years.) It was suggested that Gene should be able to set me up with a simple 90-day renewable note, which is also known as the "90-day noose." This is basically a loan where you can refresh the loan if you have paid off a portion of the loan. Borrow sixty thousand dollars in April, pay the bank twenty thousand in May, June, and July and go back for another sixty thousand or more in August.

I called Gene to set up an appointment, and found I would have to go to the main office in downtown Cincinnati. I seldom left the suburbs for *any*thing, so even going downtown was going to be an adventure. I was really impressed when I walked in to the skyscraper and finally got to Gene's opulent office, nicely furnished, with a great river view. It certainly looked like they had plenty of money, but I felt out of my league and I figured my chances of getting a loan were going to be nil from this stranger. I wished I had worn a tie.

Gene put me at ease by complimenting me on the successful growth of our business. He looked over my financial statements and helped me fill out the application on the spot. He pointed out how much our asset base had increased in just the last three years then said, "We would like to become a partner in your future growth."

He spent most of his time just being nice, asking about my college years, how I had gotten interested in being involved in the family business, and so on. He seemed genuinely interested in being my buddy. He let it be known that they would like to be our bank and take care of ALL of our banking needs. Finally, he said he would let me know in a couple of days the results of our loan application, but he did not foresee any problems.

I am not sure what the law was in 1976, but I do not think a bank can require you to move your deposit business as a condition of the loan. I learned a lot about "tying" and other anti-trust issues as a defendant in a suit that was filed against me for "monopolizing" the sale of sewing machines in our market area. I do know that if you are willing to move your deposit business to the bank from which you are seeking the loan it will certainly lubricate the process. I was so furious at my original bank for treating me like I was some kind of a fool, that I told Gene I would gladly let him handle all of our business.

Within two days I had a new checking account and the loan I needed with a very small mark up over prime. My rate was almost as low as what my business neighbor in Cincinnati, Procter and Gamble, was paying. I now had to drive a half-mile every day to make deposits rather than walk across the street, but the savings on the loan were well worth it.

The Business of Borrowing

I might have thought this was a one-time fluke and would not have written this chapter if I had not run into a very similar scenario on at least two other occasions as I was building my chain of retail stores. Each time, I would first attempt to borrow from my current banker for the store or the corporation that needed additional working capital. Each time, I received a kinder, gentler offer from a bank that was out hustling for new customers.

Many years later I reverted back to the original bank, which was then operating as PNC bank, and the cycle repeated itself. One of my branch locations was enjoying unusual success and needed more operating capital to cover the high levels of inventory and accounts receivable that supported the increased sales. A new multiple year relationship had been established with PNC bank.

This time the transaction became more of an underwriting nightmare. The loan officer kept asking for more and more documentation. It started out with just requests for the corporate entity that was going to be borrowing the money. When it was expanded into a request for financial information from two of my other related corporations, my frustration tolerance had reached its limit.

It was ironic that a new bank in town had a representative going door-to-door calling on all businesses in the area. It was a very low keyed approach, "Hello, I am Mike from Huntington Bank. We are new in your neighborhood. Here is some information on our business services. Give me a call if I can ever be of assistance. Have a nice day, goodbye." I had to follow him out to the parking lot yelling, "Wait! Wait!" I caught up with him. Within three days, I had the bank loan I needed, at the rate I was seeking, and Huntington Bank had a new customer.

Let the Buyer Beware

In theory, you would think that your banker would be your best buddy. I say, "Beware!" Go ahead and make your request with your current bank, but always be prepared to shop around for your banking services no matter how long you have had a working relationship with your current financial institution. My experience on these and many other occasions clearly demonstrates that there is a high likelihood that a bank looking to add customers is going to have the friendliest loans and deals.

In the first example, I found that I was much better off going downtown directly to the commercial loan department rather than the suburban branch manager. A local branch manager generally has limited authority to loan money compared to the specialized loan officers at the main location where large loans will most likely have to go for approval.

I had the same experience with credit card deposits. A new bank in town offered me a significantly lower charge to process credit cards than my existing bank. What's the big deal about a half of a percentage point? The big deal is that by lowering my rate from 2.3% to 1.8%, my cost to accept credit cards dropped by 21.7%. I had to open a new account, yes, but tremendous savings offset that slight inconvenience.

Credit card services are highly competitive, and filled with smoke and mirrors. Shop carefully. You are seldom comparing apples to apples and you MUST consider many factors besides the simple discount rate.
- Is there a per transaction charge?
- Is there a per deposit charge?
- Are you going to buy or lease the transponder, which verifies the credit cards and sends the deposits to the bank or processing center?
- How quickly is the money made available to you in your account?
- Is the rate the same for both credit and debit cards?

Going In Debit

My editorial comment on debit cards is that *they* are the bank's best buddy. The consumer who uses them is a sucker because he now loses the float time provided by a credit card. The merchant loses because if you think of the transaction as a check, you are now paying/giving the bank 2 to 3% on every "check" payment. Again, you must think of the percentage of the percentage. If you have been operating on a net profit of 5% and suddenly 50% of your transactions are with debit cards, which cost you 2%, the bank will be eating 20% of your bottom line just to service the debit cards. With friends like that, who needs competitors to run you out of business?

Wal-Mart saw the scam immediately and filed suit against the major credit card companies. Like most suits of this type, it might not be until the fifth printing of this book until we learn the final outcome, but this time I am rooting for Wal-Mart.

In Sum

A retired banker friend of mine reviewed this chapter for me. His main reaction was sadness about my personal experience with banks. He said it shouldn't be that way. Ben is a nice person, and I am sure he was a nice banker. Based on my conversations with him I will reluctantly admit that my experiences may have been atypical. The reluctance in the admission comes from my three strike-downs in a row. My hope is that you have a banker like Ben. If not, look for one across or down the street. My banker now is one of my best buddies. If you shop, you CAN find a bank that will be a partner and a buddy in your business.

PART II –

LAYING THE GROUNDWORK

Chapter 5
PERSONNEL ISSUES

Employees! You must have them, but many times it is hard to love them! My frustration in dealing with personnel issues, issues between and among employees in particular, helped to propel me into early retirement. On the plus side, I had many wonderful employees who became and will always be dear and close friends.

The big questions are: (1) how do you find good employee prospects? and (2) how do you know which one to select for a pleasant experience?

A method that served me well was to maintain a prospect list chosen from my customer base. Pleasant, knowledgeable customers can easily transition into pleasant, knowledgeable employees. A case in point: I had one customer who I got to know quite well because, unfortunately, I hold sold her a "lemon" of a sewing machine. What caught my attention was the patience and nice demeanor that this young lady maintained problem after problem, trip after trip to our service department. I silently and secretly entered her name into my employee prospect database. Two years later she became part of the interview pool for a sales position that had opened and she is still with the firm today.

There are many ways to choose employees. In Chapter 2, I went into great detail about issues that should be considered if you are hiring a store manager, even though I have seen some great success with much simpler methods. One of my dearest friends for over twenty years owns a little restaurant six blocks from what was my base of operations for the same twenty years. I was a frequent diner at Kathy's Place because my body and soul were nurtured. Kathy knew almost every customer by name and greeted him or her with a hug. Her high school helpers who waited tables were pleasant and cheerful. When you left Kathy's place, you left feeling good even if you didn't have time to eat!

I asked Kathy, "How did you find such a nice group of workers?" Her reply, "I hired them on their smile. "Hire them on their smile." That simple technique worked well for Kathy, but over the years I have developed a fine-tuned hiring philosophy that should serve *you* as well.

Rule number one, the quality of the employee you hire is likely to be in direct proportion to the size of the pool of applicants from which you make your selection.

I once selected a part time salesperson from a very tiny group of applicants and it was a disaster because she turned out to be "a toxic person". Why did I hire such a loser, you are wondering? It was because I made the mistake of picking the best of three. Choosing the best from only three applicants was tantamount to picking "the cream of the crap." Do whatever it takes to get a good pool of applicants before you select your employees.

This one hiring mistake showed me how much pollution a "toxic person" can put into the work environment. She was selfish, she was greedy, she was nasty to customers, and she was lazy. When I terminated her it was like the huge dark clouds that had crept into our store left and the sun came out again. The remaining employees, including myself, were reenergized. The morale that had sunk down shot back up. Bad things can be happening to your business, but the insidious effects of a "toxic person" cause a lot of harm before you realize how serious the situation has gotten.

A corollary to rule number one is to invest heavily in recruiting for a position *before* you invest (and lose heavily) in a disastrous employee.

This is where a mindset adjustment might be needed. You decide that spending six hundred dollars ought to be plenty, and take what you can get for that. This is a perfect example of the <u>home versus business</u> disconnect that I see so often. You are advertising for a $30,000.00 per year position and you would hope that a carefully chosen employee might be with you for ten years or more. When you hire someone like that, you have just "bought" a $300,000 employee and the most "commission" you were willing to pay your advertisers for bringing them to you was $600 or two tenths of one percent. Six months ago you paid your real estate agent $18,000.00 (six percent) to unload your $300,000.00 home. I think you should see the "duh factor" at work without any further preaching from me.

Rule number two is to consider offering wages 20% higher than your competitors for a similar position. This should enable you to attract and maintain employees which are up to 200% more effective. It was W. Clement Stone who said there is only a little difference in people but this little difference makes all the difference in the world. If you hire employees with this slight edge difference, it will make all the difference in the world to the success of your business.

Sales people at Nordstrom Department Stores are paid two dollars *more* per hour than competing department stores, plus they are given an unusual 6-3/4% commission on sales. It is not an accident that they have become famous for their good customer service.

Mr. Dave Goodman, who worked with me for nearly twenty years, literally did the work of two people, if not three, without any compromise in quality. As he once observed, "Some people literally walk and move twice as fast as others." Dave was such a person. Dave annoyed his employees at times because of his ability to focus. Interruptions were not welcomed. Thus, his store and his employees profited (since he always had incentive programs for them).

Dave was respected despite his "rudeness" to employees. Part of Dave's efficiency program was to eat at his desk so he could continue working. It was during his lunchtime that he would call me to discuss business matters. I would hear crunchy sounds as part of the conversation.

I asked, "Dave, what is that noise?" He said, "I am eating Doritos." Dave annoyed me with such rudeness but I was quick to forgive him since he was making a ton of money for both of us. I didn't try to break him of the habit, but I did use my best salesmanship to persuade him to switch from Doritos to Yogurt for lunch.

I remember when Dave became frustrated with me when I was pursuing a new career as a professional speaker. He was clearly carrying more than his share of the burden for our stores when he only shared in the profits from that store which he managed. Dave took care of all of the advertising, the publishing of our newsletter, and much of the buying. Dave was more patient than I would have been in such a situation. He finally suggested that I buy back his shares of the corporation and he would open his own store outside the area governed by his non-compete employment agreement. Knowing that I would have to hire two or three people to do all that Dave was doing for our business, I ended up selling my shares to him. It was an invisible change to our customers as the stores continued with all of the joint advertising and promotions. I cashed out, and Dave now only had to split profits once with the IRS and not twice. Dave was good at making a big profit pie and he liked having a half much better than a fourth.

Since Dave was my super star employee of all time, you might be curious to know that he was found walking the streets with a degree in business management from Purdue University. Dave started his career with Procter and Gamble but after just a few years, the management versus labor issues had diminished his happiness. Dave had been a manager.

Once upon a day he walked into our store shortly after I had taken over the business and tried to sell my dad an advertisement in "TV Facts." This was a local free circulation publication modeled after *TV Guide*. Dad told him that he would have to come back and meet his son Bob, the new business owner. Dad told me about Dave and I insisted that I would not call him because I did not need to talk to any more sales people.

The first thing you will learn after starting a new business is that more people will come in trying to take money out of your cash register than come in to buy, but Dad was so impressed with Dave's personality and enthusiasm that he *ordered* me to meet with Dave. And Dave and I worked together happily ever after.

I immediately started advertising in TV Facts and Dave ALWAYS delivered more than he promised. He took the photos for the ads, helped write the copy and made sure I was happy. It wasn't long before I was opening a new store and it was me who was begging Dave to meet *with me* to discuss the possibility of having him manage the new location. So begins the end of the story.

How much do you need to pay a guy like Dave? I say pay them what they are worth and a bit more. There is a great formula for determining this which I learned early on from reading Napoleon Hill's classic, ***Think and Grow Rich***. The formula is:

$$C = Q + Q + MA$$

Your C-ompensation should equal the Q-uantity of the work which you do, plus the Q-uality of that work, plus the M-ental A-ttitude with which you render that service.

I hired a vacuum cleaner technician because of his claim that he could repair twenty machines a day on an average day but, alas, over 20% of them came back with a consumer complaint. Either they were not repaired properly or simply not cleaned satisfactorily. Nor could I afford to hire someone who would meticulously repair every unit, and polish and spit shine the vac until it gleamed if the output was only two per day. Finally I found what I thought was the perfect vac technician. He could do twelve a day properly, they went out looking good, and it was rare to have a "redo" request. I congratulated myself for hiring this excellent employee. Unfortunately, he turned into a perfect example of the "new broom sweeps clean" syndrome. He eventually lost his job with Kramer's after becoming more and more negative. Over time, his attitude deteriorated to the point he was really annoying, and demoralizing the other employees that DID have a good positive attitude. This was a person that I really liked, but he, too, ended up being toxic.

Once you have found good employees, it can be just as challenging to keep them. The simple secret is to keep your employees happy and motivated.

In a Gallup poll asking what would increase their job satisfaction, 33% said, "Let me put my ideas into action." 27% said, "Pay me more." 19% said, "Recognize my efforts more." And 17% said, "Listen to my ideas for improvement." You can raise the satisfaction of employees by paying them more, but twice as many would be happier if you simply listen to what they had to say.

Employee empowerment is

one of the most powerful aspects of the total quality management movement.

Employees want to feel appreciated. They want your applause. Use "post-it note therapy" to provide frequent encouragement, appreciation, and affirmation to your staff. I often attached a one or two phrase note to my employees' checks to remind them of how much I appreciated them. Or, as Ken Blanchard suggested, "I would catch them doing something right" and immediately acknowledge it. It's so simple; it's so cheap; it's so important. Just DO IT.

It worked for me. Here is the body of a very nice letter that I once received from an employee: *You are the very best employer that I have ever had. One of the neatest things that you do as a boss is recognizing your employee's efforts. Acknowledgements and pats on the backs that you have given me, give me the incentive to continue working hard and to give more wherever I can. I know they have also been very important to co-workers as they have shared their feelings with me. I think that this considerate action helps to maintain an atmosphere of trust and openness between you and us. I know from my own experiences that there are very few bosses that recognize the work that their employee's do.*

I was very happy to get that letter.

Unfortunately, negative situations can and will eventually occur.

What happens when you must finally part ways with an employee? You call an attorney. My worst situation was with what I can only describe as a dangerous employee who started out as my best sewing machine tech ever. He was another example of the old adage "a new broom sweeps clean." This gentleman was an extremely talented mechanic, probably the best sewing machine mechanic in the region.

Yet, he turned out to be an employer's worst nightmare. Over a period of about five years his quantity of work, quality of work, and particularly his mental attitude declined before going into a nose dive that led to the end of his career at Kramer's. Fortunately for me, and in the words of my labor lawyer George Yund, "he abandoned his job," so I never had to fire him. This was a happy ending to a sad chapter. I could not safely fire this guy. My employee was protected by our federal government with three layers of potential litigation in the event of a job termination: One, he was a Vietnam War veteran; two, he had a certified post traumatic stress disability and, three, he had reached the age of being able to file an age discrimination lawsuit. This story could become a second book, so I will share the short version.

As we later discovered, this individual had been secretly taping conversations between me and another store manager, so knew his end was near. Fortunately for us one Monday morning he chose to go to a bar instead of work. We got a call from the bar owner alerting us that he was in the bar threatening to do us in. Prepared for the worst, I quickly called my mortician and my attorney. When asked what to do, labor law specialist George Yund said, "Celebrate." "He has abandoned his job." To translate this legal phrase, it meant "Change the locks and don't ever let him back in the store." It is always better when the employee terminates the job. The chance of a successful lawsuit against the employer drops a hundred fold or more.

Chapter 6
TRADITIONAL ADVERTISING

Conventional advertising is *very* expensive. If you are going to use newspaper, TV, radio, direct mail, and/or billboards to advertise your business, do it very judiciously. My suggestion is to spend the minimum amount you can, using it optimally to get the maximum exposure. I hope the lessons I learned the hard way will help you.

Having a plan is the single most important thing a business owner can do to improve his advertising. Too many people approach their marketing haphazardly. They advertise now and then without any specific objectives, without a budget, without really thinking about what is happening or not happening. This reckless approach is wasteful and seldom produces satisfactory results. It is so much better to have a plan.

To obtain the best possible results:

1. **Determine your objectives**
2. **Establish a sensible budget**
3. **Schedule your expenditures**

What would you like for your advertising to do over the next twelve months? Increase sales 20%? Sell higher end merchandise? Make people more aware of your location? The more specific you can be, the easier it is to formulate a plan.

Investment Advertising

Your objectives will help you decide how much to spend. If you have recently relocated, added a new location, or introduced a new product, then you may wish to do some "investment" advertising. Since you will spend a lot of money in a relatively short period of time, with the hopes of receiving long-term dividends, you must decide how much you can afford to spend to get the word out.

The easiest way to establish an advertising budget is to allocate a certain percentage of projected sales. If you anticipate $100,000.00 in sales for a certain time period and decide to spend 5% of sales on advertising, then it is very simple — you have $5,000 to spend.

Your competitors may influence your budget. You can't match the giants, but you may wish to at least keep up with the other independent retailers your size. Exactly how you determine your budget is not nearly as critical as not having one!

Let's say you have decided to spend $24,000.00 on advertising in the coming calendar year. The next question is — when to spend it. Will you spend $2,000.00 each month, or spend it all in the six weeks before Christmas? The first idea is not as ridiculous as the second but neither choice is optimal. Proper timing of your advertising is important to its success. Thus, a picture of your business cycle will help you time your advertising.

Look at your January sales total for the past three or five years and find the average. Then, do the same for each month and plot the results on a simple graph. Now you can see the highs and lows of your business cycle. Why are some months over twice as great as others? What does this have to do with advertising?

Perhaps you might feel inclined to advertise more heavily during your slow months to help even out the year. Actually, it is my opinion that just the opposite approach is the most sensible. Advertise when the market potential is high. You advertise to increase your market share, so advertise when the total market is the greatest

[As an example, let's say in your market area that 1000 widgets are sold each July and you normally sell 5% or 50 of these. In November 4000 widgets are sold and you sell 5%, or 200 units. Now let's assume that with a $4,000 advertising campaign, you will be able to increase your market share by 3%. If you spend your $4,000 in July you will sell 30 additional units (3% of 1000). If you spend your money in November you will sell 120 additional units (3% of 4000). You achieve four times the results with the same expenditure because the total market is four times larger.]

This example is too simplistic to accurately represent the true market place with its infinite variables, but it illustrates why I believe this is an easy and efficient way to schedule your advertising expenditures.

Take the monthly sales totals, which you used to determine your business cycle, and compute the percent of the total yearly business that you do in each of the twelve months. You now have a straightforward way to budget the $24,000.00 which you plan to spend in the coming year. If 10% of your sales are in January, then budget $2,000.00 for January and so on.

This method of budgeting may seem too cut and dried to be much fun. If you want to play with it, then you might want to try this. On second thought, you really *ought* to try this: Lead your sales peaks by about four weeks, with your advertising. This accomplishes two very important objectives. First, you get the jump on the competition and get first crack at the consumer's dollar. Your advertising is not as likely to get lost in clutter when everyone else who is selling competitive products also starts their peak season advertising. You should emphasize layaways and deferred payment plans since you are seeking to accelerate gift buying, for example. The second advantage is that by bunching up your expenditures four weeks early you've made somewhat of a splash in the marketplace. Hopefully, your name will remain in the forefront of many consumers' minds during the actual peak season even though you will be doing very little advertising during that time.

Let's face it; good planning is an art as much as it is a science so you will need to do some experimenting to find out what works best in your situation. **The real key is to take the time to <u>think</u> <u>and</u> to *<u>plan ahead</u>*.** The exact approach you use to form your plan is secondary. Having a plan to follow can only help. If it is not working, then you can revise the plan, but without the plan, by the time you discover that what you are doing is failing, it may be too late to change. Some retailers are guilty of spending more time planning the family's annual two-week vacation than the business's twelve-month advertising plan. Don't be one of them!

Written Media

Once you decide how much to spend on advertising, and *when to spend it*, you must decide *<u>where</u>* to spend it. The variety of alternatives complicates this important decision. The balance of this chapter will discuss newspaper, radio, television, and direct mail since these are the media used most frequently. After a brief comparison of these four media, some suggestions on how to choose between different vehicles of the same medium will be offered. A special chapter of this book has been devoted entirely to newspaper advertising since it is the most heavily used for the majority of small businesses. I am not ignoring yellow page advertising. Being the monster that it is, I have dedicated a special chapter to it, as well.

I have a hunch that a large percentage of smaller retailers have limited their advertising to newspaper, and direct mail and have shied away from radio and television. In many cases, this could be the only choice, or at least the only reasonable choice. Newspaper ads are generally the easiest to prepare, they require a relatively short lead time, and the results are fairly easy to measure. Newspaper ads tend to be the most effective in eliciting a prompt response to a special promotion. Newspapers produce an ad, which can be scrutinized for a long period of time. Please refer to Chapter 7 for a complete discussion.

Direct mail is simple and straightforward, especially if you include companies like Val-Pak in the equation. These companies will produce your ad, combine it with offers from many other businesses and mail zones of

10,000. If your ad is properly prepared with a strong offer, you should get decent results. A big advantage is that you can target the neighborhoods you wish to reach. You might experiment targeting the immediate market area of your nearest competitor, since you are most likely already receiving the majority of the business from the five-mile radius surrounding your business. Why discount business that is already yours? Build market share by enticing customers away from your competitors.

My best success with direct mail was promoting the sewing machine half of my sew and vac business with an in house produced newsletter sent to a mailing list that I had carefully raised, weeded, and pruned to over 10,000. Consider this. Research told me that only one in twenty households had an active sewing machine user. Picture this. Ninety-five percent of the newspaper circulation that carried an ad for a sewing machine sale or service offer might just have well been dumped in to the sewer. The same would be true for the other media. An exception might be advertising on a cable TV sewing program.

The key to success is building a quality list, and maintaining it. I included all customers who came in to my store for any sewing machine purchase or service. Radio Shack research showed that the best prospect for a sale is the customer who was most recently in your store. When a competitor went out of business, I acquired their mailing list for a giant bottle of brandy and a few kind words. I purchased some names from a national sewing publication. More names were acquired from a promoter who sponsored a home sewing exhibition at our local convention center.

One hundred percent of the households who received my newsletter had an active interest in sewing as opposed to the five percent that other media would have reached. As in newspaper advertising, we tried to balance our newsletter with editorial and offers. In fact we called it "HINTS AND NEWS." Short articles offering tips on hemming denim blue jeans, sewing on difficult fabrics, and more, would encourage readership.

Broadcasting Media

The broadcasting media offer other advantages, which demand that the smart business consider incorporating into its advertising program. Television advertising, in particular, tends to have a longer-lasting effect since it appeals both sight and sound. Action and color add impact to the commercial message.

Television also provides prestige for your product and for your store. Prospective consumers will tend to think of you as being successful, and that you are here to stay. Even though this is not a valid assumption, it is still an advantage for the television advertiser. Television generally requires a larger budget, for both the production and the airing of the commercial.

If you wish to use television but promotional tapes are not available from your merchandise suppliers, do not count yourself out. Unless your supplier is paying for at least half of the cost, I would not use their materials anyway. **Focus on *your business* more than your product if you are using your own money.**

Inexpensive commercials can be produced onsite with video. This will allow you to focus more on your own store name, or on a special local promotion. This will more than offset the disadvantage of not having a professionally produced commercial.

If you are based in a large metro area, the high cost and large amount of "waste circulation" will make television impractical for most, but if you are in a smaller rural market and the only game in town, it might make great sense. A tire dealer friend of mine has had great success promoting his business with television. Because of our local cable franchise, he is able to advertise in his immediate market area only. He focuses on promoting fast, low-cost oil changes, yet he sells lots of tires and repair services as a direct result of his advertising dollar.

Radio advertising also has unique advantages. In large market areas, with many stations, you can be selective. You can choose the one or two stations with a listener profile that most closely matches your customer profile. In rural areas, where you have a large but sparsely populated market demographic, it might take several local papers to reach the market. If there happens to be one radio station that "everyone" listens to, radio could be your more efficient medium. A sewing machine dealer friend of mine in Detroit swore by the results he received from advertising exclusively on Christian radio stations.

RADIO & TELEVISION ADVERTISING SUPPORTS NEWSPAPER OR DIRECT MAIL ADVERTISING

A newspaper clearance sale on a specific brand of vacuum cleaner should produce more results if brand recognition has been established by the manufacturer's national television advertising campaign. Moreover, a more direct support method is to call attention to the specific ad you are running in the paper. Is it better to use one medium, or a combination of two or three? A study of your market area and the relative costs of each should help you to decide.

A critical point to keep in mind in buying broadcast time is that you do NOT compare the cost per sixty seconds on one station with the cost per sixty seconds on another station. The correct way to do it is to compare the CPM, known as cost per thousand, to reach the specific demographic profile that you are seeking. Since not all listeners are likely to patronize your store, you are better off comparing stations on their ability to reach your typical customer.

For example, if your store sells automotive parts and accessories, you want to compare stations on their ability to reach listeners or viewers who would likely shop for automotive parts and accessories. You may wish to compare the CPM's for men ages 18 to 49. Ask each of your station representatives to make this comparison for you, since they have easy access to the Neilsen ratings. You can check the comparisons against each other to see that correct calculations have been made. Ask each station to break out exactly the same group of listeners. The CPM to reach the 18-49 year-old male audience or the 25-49 year old male audience will vary depending upon the time of day, radio personality, or television program. A CPM comparison will help you select the most efficient schedule to run on a particular station.

One $200 Spot (or Two $100 Spots) May Provide Better Value Than Ten $20 spots

Do not forget to ask for special packages. Most stations are negotiable and most have multiple rate charts. The expensive chart is for the naïve. The stations have their slow seasons and can make some attractive offers when their "inventory" of unsold spots is high. Do not buy time, however, just because it is cheap. Remember, it is the cost to reach one thousand of your prospects that will tell you if you are really getting a fair and competitive value.

Network with other small business owners in your area. Talk to them; find out what is, and what is not working for them.

Chapter 7
NEWSPAPER ADVERTISING

As I mentioned in Chapter 6, newspaper is probably the most common advertising medium used by small business owners. For that very reason more money is probably wasted *misusing* newspaper advertising than in any other area.

Newspaper ads are generally the easiest to prepare, they require a relatively short lead-time, and the results are fairly easy to measure. Newspaper ads tend to be the most effective in eliciting a prompt response to a special promotion. Newspapers produce an advertisement that can be scrutinized for a long period of time. The goal of this chapter is to help you get the most for your money when you do decide to advertise in the newspaper.

The first thing you must consider when choosing any type of media is your store's trading area. For your advertising to be cost effective, you must focus your dollars *only* on the people in your true market area. The primary area for most businesses is a geographic region that extends out from the store radially from 2 to 5 miles.

To measure the actual trading area of your store, plot three hundred or more recent customers on a map. Draw a boundary around the area that includes two-thirds to three-quarters of those customers. The area within your boundary is the *primary market area* for your store. Because of highway configurations, natural boundaries, shopping habits etc., you should not expect a perfect circle. You might want to add the location of your competitors to your map see how they affect your trading area.

ALL media that you purchase should be evaluated only in terms of its penetration into this primary area. Money spent reaching people outside this area is generally wasted. As an example, let's say you have a single store, located in a suburban shopping center, in a major metropolitan market. If you advertise in the major daily newspaper, with a circulation of 400,000, the greatest part of your money is consumed reaching people outside your market area. This is seldom a smart move!

The main rule to follow is: *Choose only media that hits your primary market in a cost effective way.*

To determine the cost per person reached, divide the number of people in your primary trading area that receive the message by the cost of the media. This will allow you to compare the cost effectiveness of the different media. This is usually easier to do than it sounds, because the data you need is readily available from the media itself. Obtain the number of subscribers by zip code area, and disregard what goes outside your area.

Another step in the media analysis is to look at the characteristics of the audience you reach, versus the profile of your typical customer. If you are planning to advertise a top line sewing machine that sells for $4,500.00 and your records (or those of your supplier) indicate that these are primarily purchased by women over 45 years old, with family incomes over $70,000.00, then you need to determine the percentage of overall subscribers who match this profile. You next multiply this percentage times the number of subscribers in your area, to determine the actual number of potential prospects for your product that the particular paper or media would be reaching. Now, divide this number for various media into the cost to let you more accurately compare different media. A good radio station that reaches upper income females might be a better buy than the major daily paper. Since only about 5% of all homes have a person actively sewing, you might discover that the small number of actual prospects vs. the overall media reach makes direct mail the only sensible alternative.

For most retailers, especially for items of more general interest, like tires, light bulbs, or vacuum cleaners, newspaper can generally be quite effective. Most people who say newspaper advertising doesn't work, just don't know how to select the newspaper, the section, the day of week, the placement etc.

When choosing a newspaper, one must consider the different characteristics of the many papers available. The paper that we are all most familiar with is the major daily, which is distributed to a large metropolitan area. The Chicago Sun-Times, The New York Times, and the Cincinnati Enquirer are examples. These are published every day.

In contrast, there are the local weeklies, which are generally published once, and sometimes twice a week. They generally serve smaller towns or just certain portions of the major cities.

Another distinguishing characteristic is whether the paper is a free circulation or a paid subscription type. Always use a paid subscription paper because the circulation figures for most free papers are meaningless, since so few of them are actually read. I once offered to pay the delivery boy to NOT leave the free paper on my drive since I considered it nothing more than a nuisance. Obviously, there are exceptions. I say that with a wry grin since I now write a column every other week for just such a paper. Each Thursday the ***Fairfield Echo*** hits the driveway of every house in the City of Fairfield and Fairfield Township and is well read for local news. While it is distributed free, with a request for voluntary payment, copies in racks sell for $1.00.

A final consideration for you to factor is whether the newspaper is the standard editorial and advertising combination type, or an ad only type, commonly referred to as a "shopper". The only time I have had any luck with a shopper was if and when I could negotiate for the top half of the front page. People would notice my ad as it sat on store counters waiting to be picked up.

The only other situation where an "ad only" paper might work is to use its classified section. In using the classifieds, you are basically availing yourself for the prospect to find you, rather than hoping they will notice your display ad. And about the only time a display ad will work in a shopper newspaper is when the product is being offered below cost. Save your display ads for the papers which will *include editorial content.*

For most single store locations, a local paper (provided it is well read) will be more cost-effective than the large metropolitan paper. This is because of the reduced waste circulation. The formula used to compare pure cost efficiencies of newspapers to reach readers, without regard to where they live, is called "the milline rate", which is the cost to reach a hypothetical one million readers with one line of advertising.

To compute the milline rate, you take the cost of one line of advertising, multiply it by 1,000,000, and divide by the paper's circulation. The larger paper will always win in this comparison, and that is the very reason why you must consider many other factors.

A local weekly is a better choice than a local daily if all other characteristics are equal. Most people tend to read the major metropolitan daily for international, national, and regional news, but will pick up a local once a week for local news. Since no two papers are the same, you need to take a close look at the number of paid subscriptions for each, in your market area. Use the milline formula as part of your study to determine which is the most cost effective.

Another way to compare papers is to run a coupon (I prefer to call it a "certificate"), or some other offer, which requires the customer to bring the ad *into the store.* You can experiment by spending the same amount in two papers (getting a much larger ad in the smaller circulation paper) and the paper that brings in the most returns is the "winner". Or you can purchase the same size ad in both papers and divide your cost for each paper by the number of returns for each. The paper with the lower cost per return is the "winner".

I would repeat this type of test at least three times before making your final conclusions since "luck of the draw" position should tend to average out over three insertions.

There are exceptions to every rule, of course, but following the rules stated above should guide you to the best paper for your money.

Down to Particulars

Once you have selected the paper, you now must decide on which day of the week to run the ad, which week of the month, which section of the paper, where on the page you want your ad to run, and whether you should use color.

The three best days to run your newspaper ad are Tuesday, Wednesday, and Thursday. Thursday might be the best choice since you aren't competing with Wednesday's grocery ads, and the timing is good for weekend business. Sunday's paper might have the bigger circulation, but that paper is so large your ad is likely to get lost and not noted.

You might choose to avoid the first week of the month when people are making most of their monthly payments. If you know when the majority of your potential customers get paid, aim for that week.

The best section is ALWAYS the front section, which is the first section of the main news. A lot of retailers think sporting goods or tires belong in the sports section, and sewing machines and fabrics belong in the style section. They are wrong! **Studies show that _the main news section gets the best readership_ from all categories of readers, and *that's the place to advertise.***

Kramer's Sew & Vac was able to lock in Page Three of the Cincinnati Enquirer by guaranteeing an ad for every Tuesday. This is the best page in the paper for readership, other than the front page, which is not available to advertisers.

Internationally recognized retail marketing specialist Gary Wright* does not recommend using the local sections of large metropolitan papers. He says, "Either go in the first section of main news or find a local paper". I think that you will find possible exceptions to this rule if the local section can be purchased in a zone of subscribers near your store. Since you are targeting your area, the computations you need to do, may show that it is an excellent value. The smaller percentage of people reading this section can be more than offset by the money you will not be wasting in main news, which reaches far outside your market area.

Page position is very important. I once attended a seminar where a newspaper representative cited a report, which indicated that positioning in the paper did not affect ad results by more than 3%. I didn't listen to another word, since he had lost all credibility. If you do enough studies, you can make them say whatever you want. My personal experience has told me plenty. The top of a right hand side page is your best bet. Many retailers believe the media sales person when he says, "There is nothing you can do about position, we sell all our ads as 'run of press'." Sometimes this is true, sometimes it's not, but it is almost always *claimed* to be true. Some tough "take it or lose it" negotiating may help you ferret out the real truth. Try to work with your rep for best position.

Another way to get your ad to the top of the page is to make it very tall and thin so that it reaches "above the fold" even if placed at the bottom. This is not my choice, since it means buying more space than I generally want. Kramer's has had good luck with an ad that is two columns wide (in a six column format paper) with a height of 3 or 4 inches. Making the ad rather "squat" in shape allows you to keep it small, while you have a good chance that it will "float" to the top. A newspaper layout person stacks ad "blocks" (and usually he is working with empty blocks that show your space requirements only without copy) just like a child would stack blocks. The bigger blocks always go on the bottom with progressively shorter and narrower blocks towards the top. Since many papers use a well-shaped configuration for the editorial, with the ads to the outside, the short narrow ads just naturally fit best up towards the top. Not all papers are laid out the same, but keep the general concepts in mind and experiment.

What about color? It is a fact that color ads outsell black and white, but there are also good reasons for not using color. Most research comparing color ads to black and white ads is comparing four-color photography ads with simple black and white. Full color newspaper ads are very expensive to use and not worth the extra cost. Frequently, two color ads (black with one other color) do not significantly enhance the results, either, and the extra color used improperly can actually detract from the ad. It most cases it is best to stay with black & white. It is not an accident that very few newspaper ads have color. If it was really worth its premium, everyone would be using it, then diluting the effectives for all, leading us back to black and white.

*Gary A. Wright's research and words in putting this chapter together are used with his permission, with my thanks. G. A. Wright Marketing, Inc., 4105 Holly Street, Denver, Colorado 80216 Email: info@gawright.com

Chapter 8
YELLOW PAGES

Christmas was exciting as a kid, but it was even more exciting as a retailer. The only other month I looked forward to with as much anxious anticipation, was June: the month the new yellow page directories came out. In the case of the latter, it was "anxiety anticipation" since it was not thoughts of "sugarplums" dancing in my head as I peeked into the pages but, rather, thoughts of how big my competitor's ads would be. Did we get a good placement? Are we on a page on the right hand side? On top or bottom? And so on.

One year my stomach went into knots when, in the first position, filling a half-page of the directory, a competitor's ad glared out at me. I ran to my father, unable to conceal the horror of my thoughts of our competitor running us out of business with the yellow plague. Dad smiled and said, **"This is good, Son, and this will be *HIS* last year in business."**

And it was. Dad had seen this pattern repeated several times over in the many years of running the business before I had gotten involved. If you want to go out with a bang, the yellow pages is the place to do it. I have seen the yellow pages put *many* people out of business. Why? Because phone book sales reps have learned to play one competitor against another. It would appear there is nothing that makes them happier than if they can create a size war. Do not get sucked into that game. One year two of my competitors went with half page ads. Resisting the strong urging of my yellow page sales rep, I stayed with my modest two-quarter column ad, I thrived, while only one of my competitors survived.

This failing is similar to buying more house than you can afford. It's motivated by greed and you will lose the house. The one competitor was unable to pay for his yellow page ad, and without payment, he was blocked from being listed in the following year's directory. No listing, not enough business to cover overhead, goodbye!

By now you should realize that I acknowledge the importance and power of the yellow pages as a critical medium for all businesses. In fact, the local yellow page company ran a full-page color magazine ad picturing my store as a testimonial yellow page success story! Just how important is the yellow page directory to your business? You certainly have to be listed, but investing in a display ad is a decision you will have to make based on your type of business and some customer research.

Keep a log next to your telephone or cash register for a couple of months and ask your customers. Be careful of the question you ask. "How did you find us?" will produce a much different result than "What caused you to do business with us?" The second question is much more important. If it is a new person in town, there is a good chance that they were referred by one of your existing customers. They might have found you by going to the telephone directory, but don't give the yellow pages credit for bringing you that customer. Give them credit for the "assist" only!

Bear in mind the alphabet when naming your business, as column ads are listed alphabetically. Thus, Animal Care Center of Woodlawn would be a smarter choice than Woodlawn Animal Care Center. Also, take advantage of alphabetical listings in the business white pages. You can have multiple listings under multiple names in both the white and yellow pages. This was a technique with which I used to get great results from the telephone directories without having to pay the cost of a large display ad. I had simple one-line listings under Hoover Approved Dealer, Oreck Approved Dealer, Dirt Devil, etc. etc. I was scattered throughout the yellow pages by brand names. Each listing in the yellow pages does require an "anchor" listing in the business white pages, but the cost is very reasonable.

I have already indicated that I did purchase a minimal display ad, two or three quarter columns in size. You are punished for buying small ads by being stuck at the end of the display ads, so you need to do what you can to make yours stand out. Generally, our ads used a reserve type headline to highlight a key point, such as, FAST SERVICE, LOW PRICES, or something similar.

Not only do I respect the yellow pages, but I also think they have some of the most well trained sales people in the world. In fact, they can really mess with your mind.

As such, watch out for these scenarios:

1)   "Sir, you have been a good customer for a long time. I want to help you! Competitor X has just purchased a half-page ad, and of course ads are placed first by size and then by seniority. You have had first position for many years but you will lose that position if you do not step up to a half-page. Here is what your ad will look like. Let's run with this, okay?"

Run away from this salesman as quickly as you can. One year the number of display ads in the directory changed, and the luck of the layout cancelled the benefit of my larger sized ad.

2)   "We have added (insert option here, red ink, white background, full color, coupons, talking yellow pages and 100 more they are thinking up as I write) and you can get it for only one-fourth the price this first year."

The sting comes the following year when the sales rep shows up very close to the deadline. He lurks in your parking lot waiting to make sure that you are in the store. Once enough customers have entered and you look harried, he runs in on the commotion. Then, as soon as he can grab your ear he says,

"Hi, Bob! Sorry I am running so late this year. If you want a proof for your ad I will need it by the end of the week. Here is what you had last year; do you want to just run with this again?"

You are caught off guard because he is not trying to sell you a bigger or additional add for the first time in years. You are busy and things are not going to get any better over the next couple of days. You sign, and you are screwed. You forgot the setup from the year before. The red ink is now going to cost you four times as much, turning more of your bottom line from green to red.

You must be proactive about your yellow page advertising. You must pay close attention to all of the charges each year.

3) "Mr. Kramer, we now have this community book available to serve just people in this shopping area. You can have the same size ad as you do in our regular directory for just one-fifth the price. Just check the block here and I'll take care of it."

Such a deal! You just paid one-fifth the price for a book with one-fiftieth the circulation and one-tenth the readership. So I am saying you will get just one penny on the dollar of additional exposure for your additional cost.

4) "Mr. Kramer we notice that you are listed under 'VACUUM CLEANERS', but I could not find your listing in "DIRT SUCKERS". We added that category a couple of years ago and just a small one-inch ad there would only be an additional $32.00 per month."

I could go on for quite a while but, even if I stopped at ten, they will have ten new strategies created by the time you buy this book. You are dealing with marketing experts and highly trained sales people. Be cautious in your dealings so that you can learn without the burn.

I suspect that by now you have become frustrated with me. It seems I write testimonials for the yellow pages and then trash them. Am I for or against yellow page advertising? You probably feel that I am biased against the yellow pages. I am, to the extent that I feel they are bigger, more professional, and more powerful than most of the small business owners that they deal with.

I respect the value of advertising in the yellow pages; however, I want you to use their service in an <u>intelligent</u> way and not get fast-talked or pressured into spending more than what is prudent. The fact that I have never been without good representation in our local yellow pages should substantively answer the question.

Looking back, I know my boat would be 22-feet longer if I had managed my yellow page advertising better. I started out with small ads and they grew as my business grew. The yellow pages will tell you that my business grew as the ad grew, and there is probably some truth to that. However, in later years, I started backing down the size of my ads and my business continued to grow while my profits grew faster.

The bottom line is that I think the value of the yellow pages versus spending your money in other media … or just saving it to buy a bigger boat … is a riddle that will never be solved. Too many other variables are in play for me to give you specific advice. What type of a business do you have? If you are a plumber it might be the best and ONLY advertising you need to do!

The best advice I can give you, I already gave you at the beginning of this section. It is to establish an advertising budget for the year and decide how much you will spend in the yellow pages BEFORE the salesperson walks in your door. Say, "I have budgeted $600 a month to spend in your "REAL" yellow pages, show me how I can get the best bang for the buck."

You probably need to spend at least $100 a month in the "UNREAL" yellow pages just to have a presence. From that remark, I think you can imagine that I was not happy when multiple yellow page directories started popping up.

I can tell you how it happened in Cincinnati. For many years the Reuben Donnelly Corporation had the contract with Cincinnati Bell to print the one and only official yellow page directory. To advertise in books to the North of my market I dealt with the L.M Berry Company out of Dayton, Ohio. When Reuben Donnelly lost the contract in Cincinnati to L.M. Berry Company, Reuben Donnelly refused to leave town. They simply published a *second* yellow page directory, creating "UNREAL" confusion for consumers and retailers alike. I am not saying they are illegitimate for doing this. It might be healthy competition, but I hated it.

Normally the directory that does not have a direct relationship with the local phone company charges about half as much for the same size ad. Even if they could prove they have more circulation, it is not a bargain if they do not have the readership. I remember foolishly paying several companies to get me listed in TWO-HUNDERED or more Internet search engines. I do not care how many on-line Internet directories there are. If people only use Google and Yahoo, being listed in the other 198 has zero value.

Next time you approach your yellow page sales person, just think of it as approaching an extremely dangerous intersection before you proceed. Think of a traffic light: red, yellow, green. Yellow is caution, be very careful with your yellow page investment or you will see red, when with good judgment you could have seen green.

PART III –

FOR THE LONG HAUL

Chapter 9

PUBLICITY

At a high school reunion recently, a friend of mine said of me, "To find out what a classmate is doing you generally need to call them. In Bob's case you can just pick up the paper and read about him!"

Read All About It!

Yes, I continue to make regular appearances in the local business news, as well as less frequent appearances on our prime time local television news, and on radio programs. Perhaps this is evidence that I do fit the description of another friend when he said, "Bob you are an egomaniac with an inferiority complex." Yes, he is still a friend and I am still "whatever" *because it is good for business.*

The obviously blinding truth here is that it is always better to get news copy rather than paid advertising copy.

Here are just a few of the reasons:
- 1) it is free;
- 2) news stories get more readership than ads;
- 3) it gives your business credibility;
- 4) it has longevity, in that, you can reprint it and post it in your place of business
- 5) it is free; and, of course,
- 6) it is free.

Yes, I know I repeated myself, but the fact is you can advertise yourself right out of business because of advertising's high cost. Henceforth, I would like for you to mentally substitute the word *"promote"* any and every time the word "advertise" pops in to your mind. Advertising should be a *supplement* rather than be the major part of your marketing campaign.

Hopefully, you are now wondering how I have been able to get so much **free publicity** on TV, on radio, and in newspapers. I have made Public Relations a primary target of my efforts. To quote business speaker Tom Peters, "Ready, fire, aim!" I shoot arrows constantly at the media, not worrying about how many fall to the ground. Yes, shoot now, ask questions later. I am going to share an incident of a misfire that allowed me to re-aim and hit the bull's-eye.

When the Viking Husqvarna sewing machine company jumped light years ahead of all of the competition with the first programmable computerized sewing machine, I went wild with enthusiasm. I could type my name or initials on the small keyboard and the sewing machine would stitch it out in neat block letters. I was convinced that this technological breakthrough was newsworthy of worldwide CNN coverage. I was sure our local TV station would jump on it for "The 7 O'clock Report", a local, primetime, evening news magazine program. Once a week for about six weeks I sent press packs and reminders to the producer, to no avail. I created my own window envelope so that I could address it with a completely stitched address on a bright fabric. I heard nothing.

It was none other than singer/songwriter Mac Davis who instructed me on how to re-aim the bow and hit the bull's-eye. My wife and I attended a live concert at the Ohio State Fair. Mac had recently made a rebound with his career and he shared the story of his slump. After getting rejection after rejection of songs he had written, he commiserated with a colleague. His friend said, "Mac you are a great singer, but the lyrics to your songs are flat. You need something with a hook."

Well, that is _exactly_ *what _you_ need* to be successful in getting free press to promote your business. You need a hook! The very next song Mac wrote was "Baby, Baby, Don't Get Hooked on Me" and his career was relaunched with this best seller.

Most news is based on the themes of sex, power, and money. Monica Lewinsky created an enormous amount of "free-publicity" for President Bill Clinton. For obvious reasons, I would suggest you go down a notch or two to one of the many other news hooks. **Human interest** is always a good one.

My hook to get on "The 7 O'clock Report" turned out to be an old lady from Arkansas named Ina Skaggs. My father generally had disastrous results hiring people who walked in the door. Growing up in the family business, I recall a string of losers he hired simply because he felt sorry for them. He finally struck gold when he hired Ina. He didn't need her, he could not afford her, but he hired her because she needed a job.

Ina was a recent widow. About the same time she lost her husband, she lost her job with the Singer Sewing Machine Company. This was during the late 1960's when Singer had enforced mandatory retirement for all employees once they reached the age of sixty-five.

Ina ended up being one of the very best employees in the fifty-seven year tenure (and still counting) of the Kramer's Sew & Vac Stores. Her talent, warmth, and friendly-but-aggressive sales skills allowed her to pay for her salary several times over. Singer had trained her well before they threw her out on the street. I swear that part of Ina's success came from her bone-rattling Arkansas drawl. No matter what a customer brought to the cash register for purchase, be it bobbins, needles, or whatever, she hit them with "DO YOU NEED ANY OIL TODAY?" The way she could say *OOOYLLLLLL* was painful, and most customers bought it, just so she wouldn't ask a second time.

Ina was a star sales person. Prospects seldom walked, and if they did, it was the beginning of a sale, not the end. Ina had a policy, after showing people a machine, of calling them once a week until they either bought one or died, whichever came first. She was polite, courteous and as tenacious as my Airedale Terrier. Once Muggsy has a good grip on his end of the tug toy he will hang on until you concede. Ina hung on to her prospects until they bought.

I praise Mr. Mac Davis for teaching me the importance of having a hook, because then I knew the Ina Skaggs story would be my hook to get on our prime time TV program to promote our new computerized sewing machine.

I sent a new package of info to the local producer with a disguised return address. Inside was an outline of the Ina Skaggs story. I included a photo of Ina who, by 1979 and age 75, looked pretty much like someone who should have retired long ago. In the package I included "love letters" sent to me by customers who praised Ina for her good service and follow up after the sale.

Within forty-eight hours a film crew was at our store. They interviewed Ina, my father Carl and me, and some customers. They filmed Ina demonstrating the amazing computerized Viking to a customer. The five-and-a-half- minute report, which finally aired, concluded with a super close-up video shot of the Viking machine stitching out, "CHANNEL TWELVE SEVEN O'CLOCK REPORT."

Even at that time a sixty second prime time TV local spot went for over $800. Five-and-a-half-minutes of paid air time would have cost over well over $4,000.00. The news report was priceless. Valuing it at $20,000.00, based on its impact on our sales and reputation, would be an understatement.

The timing — right before Christmas — was perfect. The story was warm, beautiful and human. In synch with the Christmas season, the producer opened the voice over monologue with, "Suppose the most popular Santa Claus in town is forced out of work at one department store and goes across the street to become even more popular at a competing department store. This is the Ina Skaggs story…" Kramer's was portrayed as the White Knight who rescued Ina from a fate worse than death, and the Viking was portrayed as the best, most advanced sewing machine ever.

Trust me; we all had a very, very Merry Christmas that year.

Any Publicity is Good Publicity

You can get noticed and promoted by the media if you are very creative and proactive in creating news. In more recent years, my focus has been to promote Bob Kramer, the motivational business speaker. I have had great success by attaching myself to events that will attract a lot of press coverage.

For example, being a semi-finalist for the very first "Survivor Island" reality TV series was a big coup for me. I had very little desire to go to an island off the coast of Borneo to eat slimy slugs, but I was thirsty for the media attention that I knew this show would receive. My thirst was easily quenched by both of our local major newspapers.

Another excellent entrée to free press is through community involvement. Community involvement is a win-win alternative to paid advertising to get the name of your company and product or service in front of consumers. I have used it as a catalyst to create the ultimate in synergy, using it as a HOOK for free publicity.

Another Brick in the Wall

Our North College Hill location was located just two blocks from the nationally recognized Clovernook Home and Center for the Blind. All businesses in the area were asked to contribute at least $1,000.00 to help fund a major expansion and to get our name on a brick. I already owned a lot of expensive bricks, because it is hard to say no to a worthy cause. Our reputation as a caring, contributing member of the business community was one of the pillars that supported our company's five decades of growth and prosperity.

The best thing to do when ambushed with a request like this is to "file for an extension" in time to reply. My mind can be very creative if I take a proposition, add caffeine and allow it to "percolate" for at least twenty-four hours. "Eureka"! I mean Hoover, Kirby, Dirt Devil, Panasonic, you name it, and the percolator had worked.

I approached the Executive Director of the Center and the team leader for fund-raising with this proposal. "If we work together, I think I can do a lot better than giving you a $1,000.00. I am willing to donate ten percent of all of my sales and service revenue for the next three-month period on any receipts turned in to your office. You will simply need to help me get the word out, and on any sale or repair bill I will give you a 10% commission for the referral with a maximum of $200.00 per sale. Hearing "I will give you $200.00 per sale" was the hook that caused them to salivate and jump on the idea. I was selling individual computerized sewing machines for over $4,000.00, so $200 was possible."

They promoted our business in their newsletter, which pretty well covered our market area. The big bonus was when their Media Relations Director arranged for the Cincinnati Enquirer to incorporate our offer as a major part of their story covering the building project and fund- raising campaign. This type of promotion in the major daily newspaper beats anything you can buy.

I did have to draw the line when the Clovernook Center asked me to post a large sign in my store advertising my rebate offer. They didn't get it! I had offered to give them 10% of any NEW BUSINESS which THEY created for me. I DID NOT offer to give them 10% of my general revenues for three months.

A little over $3,000.00 in receipts was redeemed. I have many other charities that I was happy to give my almost $700 in savings to from the original $1000 requested. It is hard to appraise the value of my $300 investment in fulfilling our 10% rebate pledge, but I feel safe in saying it was worth at least ten times what a $300 newspaper ad would have been worth.

Chapter 10
CROSS-PROMOTIONS

Cross-promotion, like cross-pollination, is perennial as well as universal. Surely, they go back to the time of the Revolutionary War. If you bought a subscription to Benjamin Franklin's Gazette, I can imagine that you might be entitled to a free gift at Paul Revere's Silver Shoppe. Or perhaps if you bought one of Mrs. Washington's cherry pies, you might have been given a gift certificate for a 25-cent-piece with her son's picture on it … just for stopping in at Paul's Shoppe.

Fast-forwarding to the present, I credit my friends and mentors Jeff and Marc Slutsky of <u>Streetfighter Marketing</u> with teaching me "the art of cross-promotions" in a refined form. This type of marketing is so effective and inexpensive that I would be surprised if you are not already using some form of cross-promotion to build your business. For the benefit of the uninitiated minority, let me start at the beginning. Basically a CROSS-PROMOTION, a specialized technique of Networking, is when two or more non-competing businesses, that share a common customer profile, refer customers to each other.

For selling sewing machines, I partnered with fabric stores. They did not sell sewing machines and I did not sell fabric, yet one without the other is useless. To promote the sale and service of vacuum cleaners I partnered with a an upscale carpet cleaning company which targeted high end homeowners, who would pay the premium charged for a superior carpet dry cleaning service.

An ideal team of cross-promotion partners could be created with a florist, bakery, reception hall, printer, disc jockey, tuxedo rental shop, photographer, "videographer," travel agency, and a priest for hire. (If this is not making sense yet, just skip to the next chapter.)

We sold a lot of Viking sewing machines one holiday season by partnering with the Fabric Circle stores in greater Cincinnati. This was a privately owned chain of eight strategically located stores. One of the few times we felt that TV advertising paid for itself was when we used it to support the cross-promotion offering. That offer was:

"Compliments of *Kramer's*

Receive five $20 "fabric bucks" good at any Fabric Circle store with the purchase of any Viking sewing machine during the months of November and December."

Contrary to the norm and expectation, we made it clear that this offer COULD be combined with any other sale offer. Our TV spots and newspaper ads prominently featured the Fabric Circle Stores. In exchange for this windfall in publicity, Fabric Circle agreed to sell us the gift certificates for fifty cents on the dollar. My partner at the time, Dave, and I insisted that the twenty-dollar fabric bucks be numbered serially and paid for only if and when they were redeemed. I think our bottom line cost for each $100 in certificates that were distributed ended up costing us less than thirty-five cents on the dollar.

**Cross-promotions satisfy
the three C's of good marketing:
cost, control,
and credibility.**

In most simple cross-promotions, the only cost is a small bill from your quick printer, and whatever the cost of the offer is that you are making. You control the area and demographics of the recipients of your offer when you choose the location and nature of your cross-promotion partner. Credibility comes from transferring the liability for the discount or special offer to the cross-promotional partner.

In the Fabric Circle example we did not have the benefit of the third "C" since *we* were making the offer. The examples below are more typical, and show the best way to structure a cross-promotion.

New Kids on the Block

We relocated one of our branch stores to a strip center anchored by a Kroger Super Grocery Store. My store manager Dave approached the Kroger deli manager seeking Kroger as a cross-promotional partner. Dave, in his wisdom, broke the ice with a nice gift for the manager when he introduced himself as a new business neighbor in the center.

Then Dave went on with, "Would you be interested in offering all of the customers who stop at your deli for lunch meats, or for a carry out sandwich, something of additional value?"

"What do you have in mind?"

"Well, in addition to selling and servicing both vacuum cleaners and sewing machines, we also sharpen knives and scissors as a service."

"What does that have to do with my deli?"

"We would have gift certificates printed for you that said, 'Compliments of Kroger's: get two knives sharpened for free at Kramer's Sew & Vac'."

It cost very little to print a six-week supply of gift certificates. Our promotion was precisely aimed to reach only people who were already shopping at the center where our new store was opening. The perception was that the free offer came from Kroger's so there was no problem charging our regular three dollars per knife for additional knives that were brought in.

Rent for Sale

The ability to transfer the liability for the discount can be the most valuable of the three C's. A case in point was when Walden Glen Apartments near the Case Western Reserve campus offered one month's free rent with any twelve-month lease. They spent major dollars advertising this promotion in the Cleveland Plain Dealer in a desperate attempt to raise their occupancy rate to a profitable level.

The Hamilton Gardens Apartments used a cross- promotion with the Director of Housing. Our on-campus housing was under built at the time. The manager of Hamilton Gardens approached the Housing Director with a very nice offer.

"We understand that you have a shortage of rooms for your students. We would like to help. Any Case Western student who comes to us with a valid student ID will receive a free month's rent with any lease. Just give them this certificate and have them bring it to our rental office."

It worked and it cost them next to nothing.

Meanwhile, back at the Walden Glen Apartments, things were going up in smoke. Yes, new customers came in and signed a lease. Current customers came in to renew for an additional year and were rejected. "Oh, you must not have read the complete ad; this offer is for NEW renters only." Guess what? They lost more business than they gained, and all because of perception.

Hamilton Gardens waged a secret targeted campaign by using a cross-promotion. If a new student resident blabbed about the discount at the swimming pool, no harm was done. The perception was that the Housing Department at Case Western Reserve University arranged the discount, and of course only university students were eligible. Existing renters did not flee in anger

How Low Can You Go?

I remember being challenged at a vacuum cleaner dealers' meeting in Las Vegas, where I had given the keynote address on low cost marketing.

After my talk, a dealer who questioned my wisdom in offering a completely free vacuum cleaner tune-up, "Compliment's of Weickert's Dry Carpet Cleaning Service," approached me. The offer read something like this:

Weickert's would like to thank you for allowing us to professionally clean your carpets. To maintain the fresh look, it is important that you have your vacuum cleaner be serviced regularly to insure that you have a good belt, fan, and bristle strips. As a token of our appreciation, take the attached gift certificate along with your carpet cleaning receipt to any Kramer's Sew & Vac store for a free tune-up. This is a $29.95 value and your only cost would be for parts, if needed.

The question from the audience member was, "How can you afford to give away thirty dollars worth of labor?" Having spent plenty of time in therapy, I have learned to always answer a question with a question or two of my own.

"Where is your store located?"

"In Tucson."

"In Tucson, how much do your normally spend to advertise — either in the paper or in Val-Pak — to advertise your vacuum service?"

"Probably about $500."

"Okay. For the $500 you spend to advertise, how many vacs will come in for service?"

"Five or ten," you say. "You are wondering how I can give away thirty dollars worth of labor which costs me fifteen, when you are spending fifty to one-hundred dollars for the same result?"

Question answered.

And another copy of my book is sold!

Chapter 11
MARKETING

"The Wounded Rabbit" Theory of Marketing

Personal experience has to be the most impressive teacher of all time. The "wounded rabbit" theory of marketing has to be the most powerful concept that has ever passed through my mind. I learned this theory the painful way. Using it since has been anything but painful. Here is what happened:

In 1987 I was forced to close one of the four stores which I was operating at the time. I offered a "Pre Going Out of Business Sale" to the customers on my mailing list. The sale was Sunday only from noon to five.

On Monday morning, Dave, who managed another Kramer's store asked, "How did it go?"

I said, "Dave you wouldn't have believed it! There was a crowd lined up outside by 11:30 a.m. Most of the afternoon they were stacked up behind the cash register three across all the way to the front of the store. It was so crowded, one lady passed out waiting in line. We did more business yesterday than we had done in the preceding two months!"

Dave said, "Come on, you're kidding."

I WASN'T kidding!

A few years ago, I observed a similar situation in Cincinnati when three major department stores went out of business at the same time. Some fellow named George from Australia had built a huge mall, which I suspected would have problems because it was located on the West side of I-71 and most of the money lives east of it. He put a Biggs hypermarket discounter in the same center with four classy department stores.

After about eighteen months, the center went bankrupt and the newspaper announced, "Bonwit Teller, B. Altmans, and Sakowitz going out of business, 20% off all merchandise." People lined up in the cold and rain for two hours before the sale started. WHY? It was irrational! Had the consumer stopped for one second and thought, they would have realized that the normal discount at a major department store is probably 35 to 40% off list. So why fight to save half as much as they could have saved the day before?

I hesitate to make value judgments, but I can't help but think of the fox that smells a wounded, bleeding rabbit in the woods. He'll do anything to get to it. He can't resist his instinct to pounce on such easy prey. When my customers could see that I was wounded and bleeding and being forced to close a store, they pounced on me with unbelievable enthusiasm.

Trust me; there are no revolutionary ideas here. The point is that I had no idea of just how powerful a marketing force the wounded rabbit was until I had my very own personal, painful experience. The consumer enjoyed taking advantage of my distress, but I have to admit that I enjoyed selling goods such as I never would have dreamed possible. I learned to avidly seek and create distress in order to have people take advantage of me as often as possible.

I can still recall a Snuffy Smith cartoon that I read almost forty years ago. Snuffy was having a huge expensive "Going Out of Business" sign made for his general store. Neighbor Homer says, "Gosh, Snuffy, that's an awfully expensive looking sign just for going out of business." Snuffy says,

"Well Homer, that sign has to last me at least 6 years."

Look for distress in your business. If you don't have any, please call me so we can co-author a best seller. A competitor of mine SILENTLY closed a store once! I couldn't believe it! He missed a chance to stuff his account with cash.

Are you remodeling, expanding, shrinking, or moving? You can remodel each spring. All you need to do is save some tarps, old paint cans, and a few beer cans. Keep it boxed up right along side your Christmas promo materials.

I ran a classified ad for used sewing machines $29 and up and got a few calls. I quickly learned I could get lots and lots of calls by advertising "Sewing machines, unclaimed, yours for the repair cost, $29 & up. Call Kramer's Service Dept." It appears that some people seem to enjoy profiting at another's loss. Why else would we be seeing distress sale ads being pushed by the manufactures?

"Overstocked!" "Manufacturer's Goof!" "Unclaimed School Machines!" "Paint Blemish!"
"Repossessed!" "Bankruptcy Stock"!

These all connect with the Wounded Rabbit Theory of Marketing. When the consumer can smell blood, the cash register will ring deep green.

"The Sheep" Theory Of Marketing

One of the biggest sales successes of my life was selling sixteen Viking vacuum cleaners for $449.00 each, in a single evening. I did it using the sheep theory of marketing.

When the Viking vacuum cleaner was introduced, I sent a newsletter to the hundreds of people who had purchased Viking sewing machines from us. The headline said, "Purchase a Viking Vacuum Cleaner at Near

Dealer Cost." Somewhere in the fine print it explained about rebates if they encouraged others to buy. Each adult who attended the advertised "vacuum cleaner seminars" would receive a $10.00 gift certificate to use in our store. The idea was to have BOTH the husband and wife attend, and it worked, eliminating a major excuse for not buying.

I was new at selling vacuum cleaners but I had practiced and rehearsed a great one-hour pitch that effectively destroyed the idea of buying any cleaner but the Viking. On the night of my first scheduled seminar, nineteen couples were present including my sister-in-law and her husband. I sensed that at the end of the seminar when I came to the moment of truth and asked, "Well, who wants one?" it was probably going to be all or none.

I needed a shill there to break the ice and make sure at least one was "sold" so I had instructed my sister-in-law Barb to write a check, take the cleaner to her car, and drive away. The plan was for her to return the cleaner the next day and get her check back, but she got so caught up in the excitement of the seminar that she decided to keep the cleaner.

That first evening sixteen of the nineteen couples bought the Viking vac. Of the first 92 couples to attend, 74 of them (that's 80%!) bought the $449.00 vacuum cleaner. I could never have closed such a high percentage without "sheep power" working in my favor.

While people were deciding to buy, they were definitely watching and responding to the actions of their peers. I would overhear whispers like, "Look, he's a doctor, he's smart and he's buying one." Or I could sense the communication in some couples, "Look, George is buying one for Margaret, don't you love me as much?"

It really was somewhat of a panic at the end with people lining up at the cash register. I always had help writing up the sales, as I was most often stuck answering questions and helping remove the doubts of those who were slow to decide. Our special offer was good only that night, of course. If they came back within a week of the seminar, they still got a "deal" but not quite as good a deal as when making their decision right then.

Is it easy to have a success like this? I'd say no, because so far it has only happened to me once. I did use a similar program to later sell microwave ovens, serger type sewing machines and bread makers. They were successful and definitely worth running, but the crowds were never as big as for the vacuums.

An extra ingredient that helped me succeed with the Viking "vac" is that I targeted existing happy Viking sewing machine owners, so they were already sold on us and on the brand.

The best part of doing these seminars was witnessing the power of **"the sheep theory of marketing"** first hand. You can use it in ways other than group demos or seminar selling. Next time you want to run a sale, try a four-hour sale, rather than a four-day sale. Have a private "After Hour's Sale," for example, or "Open By Invitation Only," to past customers. The idea is to concentrate lots of customers into your store in a relatively short period of time to create what is called a "buying frenzy."

The best way to get most people to buy is to let them see others who are buying. People hate to make buying decisions and feel much more comfortable following the lead of others. Remember, if one sheep goes over the hill, many more are sure to follow. Whenever possible, you should plan promotions to get crowds of people into your store for short seminars or sales. You will be pleased with the results.

PART IV –

ABOVE AND BEYOND

Chapter 12
WEB MARKETING

I would be remiss to write a book discussing clever marketing strategies without mentioning the Internet. Let me start with two statements. First, this is NOT my area of expertise. Second, I have had outstanding success using it. However, my phenomenal success has been with http://www.siestakeyheaven.com Obviously this site does not promote the sale of sewing machines or vacuum cleaners. If you want to see a Kramer's site set up for that purpose, go to http://www.sewing-vac.com or to http://www.kramersews.com.

Businesses of every type and size are extremely foolish if they do not have a presence on the World Wide Web. The value of that presence will be dependant on the type of the business. To advertise and promote rentals at my Florida condo, which is my latest business success story, would not be much of a story without the leads pouring in from its website. If you have a parallel target market, which relies on attracting customers from around the world, then nothing matches the Internet for giant results from a rather small investment. My condo is booked far in advance with guests from England, Germany, Canada, as well as from all parts of the United States.

The trading radius for my condo rental business could be described as 3,960 miles, the mean radius of our earth. For each Kramer's Sew & Vac store, the effective trading radius shrinks 99.49% to twenty miles. Almost by definition, the power of the web to create sales expands by a similar amount.

Can any small business benefit from a web presence? Is it really worth the investment? Yes and yes are the correct answers.

First of all, the investment does not have to be very large. To register and maintain a domain costs no more than $35 a year. Site hosting typically costs between $15.00-$30.00 a month. The charges can and will run much higher for a large, complex site, requiring a lot of storage space on the host computer. You can easily be up and running on the Internet for less than five hundred dollars. If you want a site like GM.com, which you do not need, then be prepared to shell out a half million dollars or so.

The Kramer's stores use the web to support sales more than to create them. Once a contact has been made in the store, or with some other promotional means, customers can then be referred to the website for additional information. After a customer has purchased a sewing machine, the website is always available to provide information on the current offering of sewing classes and seminars. Customers can check on new products and accessories designed to enhance their initial purchase as they become available.

The manner in which you set up and promote your website will be determined by the type of business you wish to support. Do you have a book to sell, book editing services, unique nautical antiques, or any other product or service, which can be delivered economically either through the electronic medium or parcel shipping?

A yes answer means you will want to design your web site to contact prospective customers. To do this you need to be easy to find.

The beauty of the web is that qualified prospects come searching for you. However, this is truly a case of classic "needle in the haystack" situation since hundreds if not millions of others may be vying to be noticed by the same prospects. You can make your "needle" easier to find if you have it "stick out", "shine and sparkle" or add some "magnetic" properties to it.

My condominium really is one of millions listed on the World Wide Web, one of thousands in Florida, and one of hundreds in the Sarasota area. In spite of these odds, several people contact me every day. This is more than enough to keep me as fully booked as one could expect.

How do they find me quickly, before they find my competitors? First, there lots of legitimate "tricks" and techniques to have your listing appear in the top five of five hundred or top five of five thousand when people do a search. I have already disclaimed my expertise in this area, but now that you know the techniques do indeed exit, I admonish you to go find them. I copped out and paid for strategic alliances with people who know the tricks. To get people to http://www.siestakeyheaven.com I paid for listings on four other sites set up to promote vacation rentals on the Gulf coast of Florida. They find these first and are only one click a way from my website.

Of course, I do some clever things of my own, like subliminally embedding an "ad" about my Little Slice of Heaven in this book, and in many other places.

Every day I get between four and eight envelopes with PREPAID POSTAGE addressed to a bank trying to sell me a credit card. Every day I mail out between four and eight business cards advertising my condo, which I get printed for free at www.vistaprint.com. My "free" bet is that the people who open these envelopes both take vacations and know people who do!

Every email which I send out is "stamped" with a signature file with a "hot link" to both my condo and to my speaking and training website at

http://www.keynoteman.com

I write a column for our local newspaper every other week and the email address which I have chosen to list at the end is bob@siestakeyheaven.com Somehow a lot of stories from my Florida visits seem to find their way into my column as well.

Once someone "visits" your website, you have perhaps three or four seconds to keep them or lose them. A website should be set up using the time-tested formula found in the acronym for writing an effective print ad:

"AIDA" = Attention, Interest, Desire and Action.

Many websites fail because they try to make the homepage too fancy with excessive graphics, and perhaps music.

Keep in mind that as this book was being written, about half of the people in the U.S. access the Internet with relatively slow dial-up phone modems. Even with my cable connection, which is approximately ten times faster than the fastest dial-up connection, I find myself skipping over many websites because I lack the patience required to wait for the first page to load.

Once you have grabbed a person's interest with a simple but catchy home page, they are much more likely to be patient to wait for subsequent pages to load. You may even issue a warning that certain links will require more time to view. This is what my son, Todd did in designing my websites. For example, if a visitor with a dial-up connection does not care to wait, they can simply skip over the icon, which would allow them to scroll around inside my condo for a 360-degree view of the interior. They can move right on to the slide show of still photos, which will load much more quickly.

Everything you need to know about designing and implementing a very effective website for any type of business is available *for free* by simply searching the Internet. If you enjoy hunting for lost coins on the beaches of Florida then you might enjoy spending endless hours searching for these golden nuggets of wisdom on the web. Personally, I prefer to ride my motorcycle, so I hire people like my son who have already located and bookmarked the location of these nuggets.

Find an expert to help you with the Internet for a very low cost.

I suggest you start first by checking with acquaintances under the age of thirteen. Bargains can still be had up through college age. Find a college student who can make the development of your website a class project and you are likely to get an A plus job!

Chapter 13

SELLING YOUR BUSINESS

At some point you will want out of your business. You will have had enough! Hopefully that "enough" included ample profits along with the normal headaches that all business owners endure, and hopefully before burn out sets in.

The big question will be, "What is my business worth?" The answer is pretty simple. It is worth the amount where the least you are willing to sell it for meets the most that a buyer is willing to pay. If these points do not meet, you do not have a sale. You either lower your price or seek a more motivated buyer.

Do not be surprised if you are unable to sell your business for what you consider it to be worth. It is my guess that, in most small business sales, the buyer will get the better deal. The "fear factor" of starting or buying a business will limit the number of prospects and depress offering prices.

I urge you to not "give" your business away. This is more likely to happen if you have kept it long after burn out has set in. You might feel like you want out at any price, so do not ever let it reach that point. Emotionally, I was at this point when it came to selling my final store. My attorney became my voice of reason.

He said, "Bob, you may not enjoy the business anymore. You may be extremely anxious to retire, but do not let that determine your asking price. Keep in mind that this business has been providing a nice income stream for you and a comfortable life style. You worked hard to build it. Don't pitch it just because you are tired of it." This little pep talk probably paid for all of Dan's legal fees, and more, in negotiating and writing the sale contract.

Assuming you are not desperate but are willing to wait for a fair offer, you must determine what a reasonable buyer should be willing to pay. You may think you can get a rough idea by comparing it to similar other businesses that have sold recently. This method might work in appraising homes where properties are similar enough, but it is not very useful in appraising a business. I am not sure why I even mentioned it, except perhaps so that I can make my suggestions (which follow) seem brilliant in comparison.

Calculate its Worth

The easiest valid method to use is to incorporate a multiple of the business' annual profits in to the formula to determine what it is worth. To start, you might say, 'I want the "book value" of my business plus three times the average earnings.' You could determine the "average" by just doing a simple average of the last three years, or look at the last five years and throw out the best and worst year and average the other three. No matter how you determine a fair value for your business, the ultimate value will be what another party is willing to pay.

It might be helpful to share how my last two sales played out.

Dave the Dependable

In situation number one the store manager had worked as an associate for over twenty years. He bought a very few shares of the corporation early in the relationship but never increased his ownership. Early on we agreed to a "split the pot" share of profits on top of his minimal salary which was tied to the consumer price index. In other words the buying power of his salary was stable for the entire time he was store manager. He earned bigger and bigger bonuses by growing the business and increasing the bottom line over the years. He was good at it, so we both benefited.

In the last couple of years before he suggested that he might want to buy the business, he had become justly frustrated with my burnout. I was spending more and more time speaking at conventions, and doing training programs for the SkillPath Seminar Company. Dave became more and more frustrated because he could only go to the bank with about one-fourth of the profit pie he created each year. After I ate my half as the founder and owner of the business, the IRS ate almost half of his half leaving him with a quarter of a pie. If he was going to continue to work hard at building the business, he wanted at least half a pie. I couldn't argue with the logic.

As most buyers and sellers do, Dave and I had vastly different ideas on what the business was worth. Perhaps it would be more accurate to say that I wanted as much money as possible and he wanted to spend as little as possible. No rocket science here, as this is true of every transaction.

I sensed that the two of us could have debated into eternity what it was really worth, and might have ended up hating each other without ever making a deal. This would have been tragic, as we had enjoyed a wonderful business relationship and friendship for years. I simply said, "Dave I will sell you the business for exactly what it is worth so that we will not have to argue about price. We can determine *exactly* what it is worth by hiring a professional small business appraisal company to set the value." I think we agreed to split the three or four thousand-dollar charge to have the appraisal done, but it was the best money spent, as it was the key to making the deal float.

After spending all of that money, we found out that there is no "exact" value. The appraisal company used three different methods to value the business. They came back with a value range between X and X + 25% dollars. After a little bit of fussing, we just agreed to pick the price right in the middle of the range.

Negotiations over?

Think again.

They had just begun.

Structure of the Sale

How a sale is structured can greatly impact the real cost to the buyer and the real after-tax gain to the seller. It is to the benefit of the seller of a closely held corporation to sell the stock and not the assets of the corporation. I am not going to go into the details of why, because I forget, and at this point if you do not have an attorney helping you, you should. Ask him.

I got my way, and it was a stock sale, but I did make multiple concessions in the structure of how I would receive payment for the business, which saved Dave a small fortune in taxes. I was highly motivated to have Dave own the business for several reasons and did not mind compromising. I knew I would not get the business back. In most of the cases where businesses like mine had been sold with seller financing involved, the new owner ran it into the ground and eventually defaulted on the payments. The original owner had to take his business back after it had been plundered. Selling to Dave eliminated this major risk. Dave had a twenty-plus year track record of exemplary store management skills.

Another reason I was fairly pliable in making concessions with Dave is that I almost felt guilty since he was paying a premium for the business because of his hard work at building it into a very profitable business. Both of us had been fairly compensated over the years, but I still felt like Dave had paid twice — once with hard work and again with cash.

I was satisfied selling the business for the value established by the appraisal company and being able to have the tax benefits of selling the shares of stock rather than the assets of the corporation. Dave had a huge smile at closing because I agreed to the structure that allowed him to pay for over half of the business with pre-taxed profits. In other words, various agreements were incorporated into the sale that allowed Dave to charge his payments for the business as expenses to the business.

How do you do this? Ask Dave, and he would say, "You play golf with a bunch of smart business people that know these tricks." Then you work with a good business attorney who can make these aggressive tax strategies safe against the sharks at the Internal Revenue Service.

I signed a non-compete agreement with Dave for which he paid me Y dollars a year for five years. I also signed on as a "consultant" for X dollars per year for five years. I took the bite on the taxes that Dave saved, since I was receiving a payoff for my business in the form of ordinary income rather than capital gains. The balance was paid to me in cash down and in the form of a note that I financed.

I wish Dave had not been so resourceful as to research his options on the golf course, but I had to admire him for it. I always admired Dave. Over twenty years Dave had earned the right to own the business which he had built, so I could easily rationalize the cash cost to me to make the sale happen. I have no regrets, nor does Dave. He sold the business just five years later at a significant gain, which once again he earned. Once he only had a single partner (the IRS) to split the pie with, he went from Mach five to warp speed in building both sales and profits. When he went to sell the business, a similar multiple of earning was used to value the business but the earnings were much higher.

Lisa the Lively

The sale of my final store occurred just four years ago. I bluffed my way into a sale out of total burnout and frustration.

At the time, I had a highly energetic sales clerk that my store manager had hired. She was making a measly amount as she had only been with us a short time, and she worked part-time without benefits, but Lisa had hyper energy and off-the-wall initiative to get things done. She was highly skilled as a seamstress, and possessed advanced computer skills. This was the ideal skill set for a business owner specializing in selling high-end sewing machines that had been designed to interface with personal computers.

At the level of burnout I had reached, I was not motivated to keep up with the operation of the scanners, digitizers, atomizers, or whatever that stuff was that was coming as 'add on accessories' to the machines. Lisa loved this stuff. In fact, she loved my business more than I did.

When I would make a rare appearance in the store, maybe once a week, Lisa would corner me with questions. "What is your vision for this store?" "What is your mission?" "Are you going to offer sewing classes this fall?" "Are you going to install a point of sale system?" It was annoying to me, so I started showing my face only once every other week. But Lisa is a very bright young lady and saw only the potential growth that was stymied by my lack of interest. She was relentless.

Finally, one day when I was totally exasperated, I gave Lisa a piece of my mind. "Look," I said. "I have operated this business profitably for over twenty-five years. I have no vision. I have no mission. Everything that you are suggesting that I do is going to have to wait for a new owner. I have been there and done most of it many times over. WHY DON'T YOU JUST BUY THE BUSINESS?"

Within three months we had closed on the sale.

Even though this sale was structured completely differently, I think it was fair and equitable. I basically used the professional appraisal that was done for the first sale I mentioned, as a model for establishing the value of *this* business.

In my sale to Dave I was willing to take a share of the PROFITS for the five-year period following the sale as part of the payment. In the case of Lisa and her husband, I had suggested that part of my compensation be based on their cost of goods. Lisa and Joe wanted it based on profits. We did neither. My CPA agreed with me that basing it on profits with a couple that had limited experience with this type of business would not be prudent. He suggested that I take a percentage of the gross revenues.

In valuing the store sold to Lisa, I had established a figure for the net worth of the business, which included items like the fixtures and equipment, the inventory, the accounts payable, and any other tangible assets. The face value of the accounts receivable were adjusted down slightly to anticipate some being uncollectible. A lot of the old parts inventory that had accumulated over fifty years of over-buying and poor inventory management was valued at zero dollars. I had paid thousands for these parts, but I could not expect a new buyer to pay for my stupidity and poor management.

The agreed upon selling agreement was very logical. I sold the tangibles for a fixed cash amount. Part of this was paid with a cash down payment; the larger part was covered with a ten-year note, payable to me at a fair interest rate.

The goodwill or intangible value of the business was based on a multiple of the average earnings of the business. Lisa, Joe and I did a forward projection of the store's sales over the next ten-year period. A scheduled small percentage payment of the sales over the next ten years was established which would pay me the multiple of earnings which I was seeking.

A third part of this transaction was a lease agreement for the property, which I owned, which housed the business. The sale of this store supported my early retirement with three income streams, monthly note payments, monthly lease payments, and quarterly good will payments based on the prior three months sales.

Both of my recent business sales were win-wins. Proof is that Dave is still one of my very best friends, and Lisa and Joe have become very, very good friends. I agreed to sell at the price I did to Lisa since there were no "tricky" consulting agreements that would inflate my annual income tax. The irony is that I have been a very active consultant to Lisa, and I didn't do squat for Dave.

Even though I have sold the business, I am happy to be involved as a sounding board for Lisa. Lisa has done extremely well in improving the store operations and in building sales. It has not been without a price to the bottom line at times; it has not been done without the stress that all business owners endure. But it is certainly a success story that I am proud to be included in.

More importantly, I know my Dad, who founded that business, could not be more pleased being able to look down on the continued success of his business. Kramer's customers continue to get "Kramer Care" even without the Kramers.

ABOUT THE AUTHOR

Bob Kramer is a former instructor of Small Business Management at Xavier University, where he received his Master's degree in Marketing. However, Bob's *real* wisdom did not come from Xavier or the business school at Case Western Reserve University where he received a B.S. degree in Management Science.

Bob's experiential wisdom came from combining his Mensa aptitude with his fighting spirit, emulating the attitude of the colonial soldier in outwitting the biggest and toughest of competitors with his own small chain of stores.

Since 1987 Bob has shared his learning experiences as a small business owner to dentists, doctors, chiropractors, hardware storeowners, swimming pool dealers, car dealers, and accountants from Canada to the Costa Del California.

Contact author at:

Robert Kramer
The Revolutionary Retailer
5690 Genevieve Place
Fairfield, OH 45014-3706

1-800-2KRAMER
keynoteman@keynoteman.com

www.ingramcontent.com/pod-product-compliance
Lightning Source LLC
Chambersburg PA
CBHW051432280526
45785CB00003B/1265

* 9 7 8 1 4 1 8 4 1 6 5 7 7 *